IMAGES
of America

MIDDLETOWN

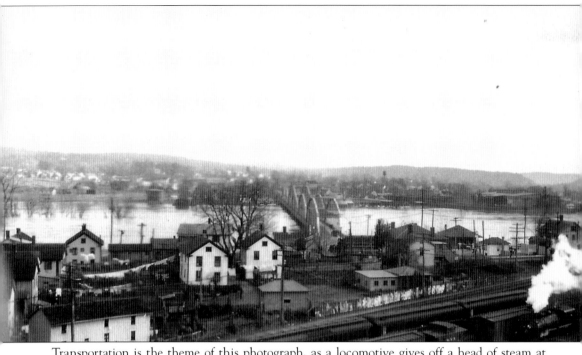

Transportation is the theme of this photograph, as a locomotive gives off a head of steam at the railroad yards by Middletown Union Station. The 1896 pedestrian bridge in the center connected Middletown with Portland on the far side of the Connecticut River. Mostly Irish immigrant families lived in the north end residences that are visible in this photograph.

On the cover: This is a view looking south on Main Street around 1920 from a point just north of Washington Street. The steeple of the South Congregational Church is visible in the distance. Various modes of transportation are clearly shown: trolley tracks, automobiles, and, in the distance, a horse-drawn wagon. (Courtesy Middlesex County Historical Society collections.)

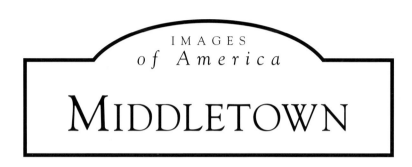

IMAGES
of America

MIDDLETOWN

Robert Hubbard, Kathleen Hubbard, and
the Middlesex County Historical Society

ARCADIA
PUBLISHING

Published by Arcadia Publishing
Charleston SC, Chicago IL, Portsmouth NH, San Francisco CA

Printed in the United States of America

Library of Congress Catalog Card Number: 2008934836

For all general information contact Arcadia Publishing at:
Telephone 843-853-2070
Fax 843-853-0044
E-mail sales@arcadiapublishing.com
For customer service and orders:
Toll-Free 1-888-313-2665

Visit us on the Internet at www.arcadiapublishing.com

CONTENTS

ACKNOWLEDGMENTS

We would first and foremost like to recognize the assistance of Donna Baron, executive director of the Middlesex County Historical Society. We were fortunate to work with a woman whose love of history is equaled only by her vast knowledge. To discuss Connecticut history with Donna has been one of the great pleasures of this project.

We would like to thank William Ryczek, president of the Middlesex County Historical Society, for his encouragement and his careful review of our manuscript. We would also like to give thanks to the following individuals who kindly provided information for the book, Vincent Cahill, Jeff Fine, Deborah Frattini, Warren Hubbard Jr., Anne Toczko Nowakowski, Robert Polselli, Denise Russo and her staff at the Russell Library Reference Department, and Suzy Taraba, Wesleyan University archivist. Many thanks also to Hilary Zusman of Arcadia Publishing for immediately answering all questions and providing valuable advice.

Unless otherwise noted, all images are from the collections of the Middlesex County Historical Society.

INTRODUCTION

Middletown is situated at the only major bend of the Connecticut River in southern New England and the place where the depth of the river dramatically declines. These facts have resulted in its importance as the site of a Native American village, its selection as one of the first English settlements in Connecticut, its position in the 1700s as the wealthiest and most populated Connecticut city, and its status as the most important seaport between Boston and New York.

In the early 1600s, the local Native American tribe, headed by Chief Sowheag, used the word *Mattabeseck* for the Middletown location. In 1650, English families from Hartford moved into the area and renamed it Middletown because of its location halfway between Saybrook, at the mouth of the Connecticut River, and the first Connecticut settlement at Windsor. Middletown originally included the present towns of Portland, East Hampton, Cromwell, Middlefield, and part of Berlin. Since large ships could not navigate the shallow waters of the river beyond Middletown, the city was the final stopping point for sea traders to the West Indies and other ports throughout the world. Shipping magnates built mansions with their earnings, a few of which still stand today.

Middletown played an important role in the struggle for American independence, as leaders like Col. Return Jonathan Meigs and Gen. Comfort Sage fought for separation from Britain. Also the city possessed a lead mine that provided material for the manufacture of ammunition.

As shipping declined in the early 1800s, Middletown turned to manufacturing and achieved a new success. In 1870, there were over 130 manufacturing companies in Middletown, which included the production of textile products, machinery, tools, and marine hardware. Prior to 1800, the population of Middletown was almost exclusively English and African American. The influx of European immigrants in the 1800s and early 1900s provided the labor force that the new factories required. First the Irish came and settled in the north end of the city, then the Germans and the Swedes. When Jews came, they settled in the southern part of Middletown, as did the Poles, while the Italians chose the center of town. At the end of the 20th century, Hispanics and people of Asian origin moved in to make Middletown their home. Each wave of immigrants has enriched the city so that today one finds a rich diversity that is sometimes matched but rarely excelled by any other city in the northeastern United States.

Education has been important to Middletown since the first schoolmaster was hired in 1675 at £20 per year. The one-room schoolhouse gave way in 1916 to consolidation of the grammar, middle, and high schools, educating many lifelong residents. In 1831, Methodist leaders founded Wesleyan University, and ever since, Middletown has been a center for higher education. Wesleyan has always ranked as one of the top liberal arts schools in the nation.

Middletown has been home to an unusual number of celebrated figures. Revolutionary War hero Col. Return Jonathan Meigs and World War II Maj. Gen. Maurice Rose were both born in Middletown. Meigs led a successful raid on Long Island–based British forces that allowed the colonies to have access to foreign goods, while Rose, who became the army's highest-ranking officer of Jewish descent, personally led Patton-like advances into Nazi Germany. Middletown was also the home of War of 1812 hero Thomas Macdonough and Civil War Gen. Joseph K. F. Mansfield. As the American naval commander at the Battle of Lake Champlain, Macdonough led the forces that captured the British fleet and prevented a British invasion of New York State. Mansfield was shot and killed by Confederate troops at the Battle of Antietam. Both were interred in Middletown, Macdonough in Riverside Cemetery and Mansfield in Indian Hill Cemetery. Middletown is the birthplace of Pres. Harry Truman's secretary of state, Dean Acheson, and became the home of Pres. Woodrow Wilson when he was a Wesleyan University professor. In addition, it is the birthplace of Willie Pep, one of the greatest prize fighters of all time, Tony Pastor, a big band leader, and Allie Wrubel, an Academy Award–winning songwriter.

Two important physical features have had a significant impact on Middletown since its founding over 350 years ago, the river and its Main Street. As demonstrated in this book, the river brought great prosperity to the city and its people, but in times of flood and hurricane, it could bring disaster. Since the founding of the 1650 meetinghouse in the middle of what would someday be Main Street, this has been at the heart of the city's economic, civic, and religious life. As Middletown's Main Street is one of the widest streets in New England, it has always been the location of dozens of retail establishments. Like bookends, two churches, one Catholic and one Protestant, stand with their tall steeples at each end of Main Street. Most of the city's other churches and its synagogue are within one block of Main Street.

While the Connecticut River gave a youthful Middletown a considerable advantage in creating opportunities for worldwide commerce, it also made Middletown's leaders reluctant to readily embrace other modes of transportation. Until the late 1800s, individuals and horse-drawn vehicles used ferries to reach Portland and other destinations on the east side of the Connecticut River. Later the railroad bridge and, a quarter century afterwards, the first pedestrian bridge made those locations accessible to railroad and motor vehicle traffic.

Although not figuring as prominently in the city's recorded history, the outlying areas of Middletown, Maromas to the south, Westfield to the west, and Staddle Hill along with Long Hill to the southwest, have been important agricultural areas.

At 44,000 inhabitants, Middletown today is the largest city in Middlesex County. It is a major college town, a thriving commercial center for surrounding communities, and an attractive location for people seeking a home in central Connecticut.

One

THE RIVER AND THE BEGINNING

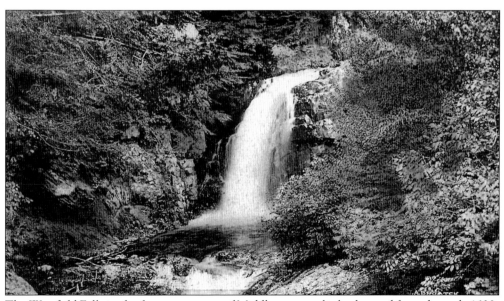

The Westfield Falls in the far western part of Middletown are little changed from the early 1600s when Native Americans had full possession of the lands of Central Connecticut. At the great bend of the Connecticut River where the city of Middletown now lies, they inhabited both sides of the river and had a major settlement on the high, easily defensible hill to the west that is now the site of Indian Hill Cemetery.

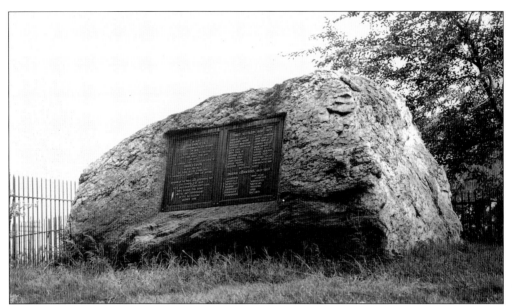

In 1900, a plaque was placed on this memorial boulder outside of Riverside Cemetery. It reads, "In 1639 Mattabeseck is first mentioned in the records. In 1650 the first English settlement was made near this spot. In 1653 the General Court changed the name to Middletown." Listed on the right side of the plaque are the names of the 13 Native Americans who granted the land and the 23 first white settlers.

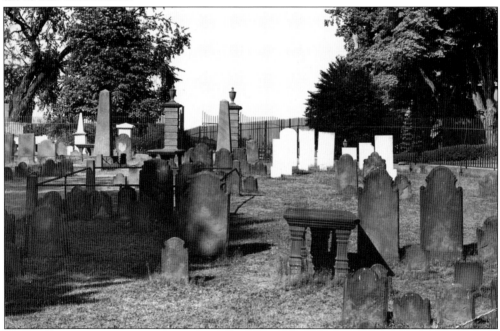

The Riverside Cemetery lies between the north end of Main Street and the river. During the first year of settlement, English families from Hartford built a meetinghouse near the entrance to this cemetery. Of the first settlers, Thomas Miller agreed to build a gristmill, William Smith to run a ferry, and George Hubbard, the official Indian trader for Mattabeseck, to keep the meetinghouse.

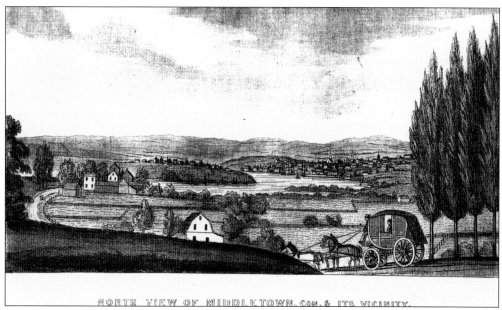

NORTH VIEW OF MIDDLETOWN, CON. & ITS VICINITY.

This view of Middletown from the north side was created by J. W. Barber in 1836. In his first visit to Middletown on October 19, 1789, George Washington noted in his diary, "we arrived at Middletown on Connecticut River being met two or three miles from it by the respectable citizens of the place, and escorted in by them. While dinner was getting ready, I took a walk around the town, from the heights of which the prospect is beautiful."

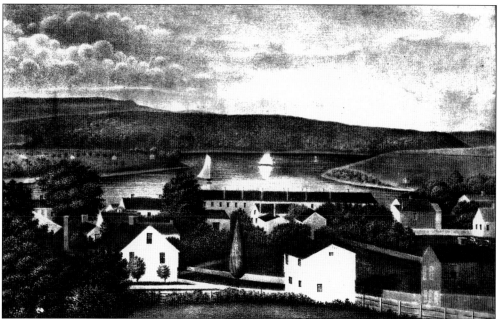

The great bend in the river can be seen in this early painting. When John Adams passed through Connecticut in 1771, he wrote in his diary, "Middletown, I think, is the most beautiful town of all. When I first came into the town, which was upon the top of a hill, there opened before me the most beautiful prospect of the river, and the intervals and improvements on each side of it, and the mountains, at about ten miles distant, both on the east and the west side of the river."

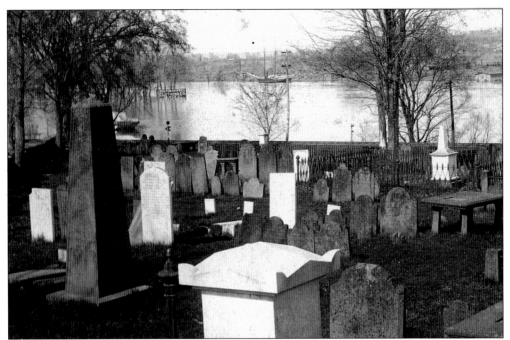

Riverside Cemetery was laid out in 1650 and is the oldest in Middletown. Before 1713, both Portland, the town across the river, and Middletown used this cemetery. However, no one could cross the river during the winter of 1713, so the Portland settlers began their own cemetery near the brownstone quarry. Brownstone from Portland's quarry was used for most of the slabs and table stones in this cemetery and can be seen in this *c.* 1890 photograph.

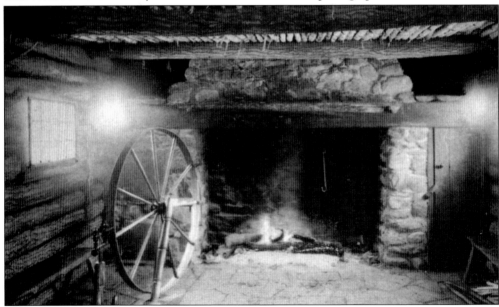

This postcard was prepared for Middletown's tercentenary celebration in 1950. It shows the interior of the cabin used as the celebration's headquarters. Representative of early dwellings, the hearth is made from local brownstone slabs and the fireplace of local fieldstone. Hand-hewn oak makes up most of the flooring.

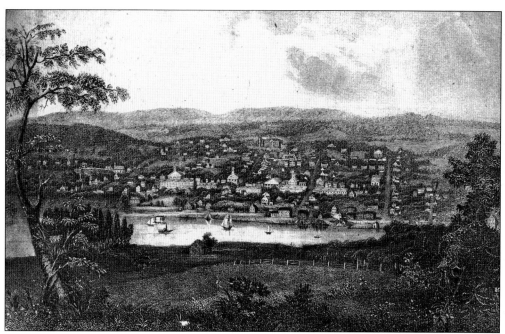

Brig. Gen. Joseph K. F. Mansfield served the army for 40 years and died in 1862 at age 59 at the Civil War's Battle of Antietam. This is a cover for sheet music titled "Colonel Mansfield's Native Home March," which was composed by Jonathan Ramsay in 1893 and dedicated to Ramsay's friend, Edward C. Hubbard Esq. of Middletown. This view shows outlying farms and a thriving town on the river supported by river traffic from New York City and Hartford.

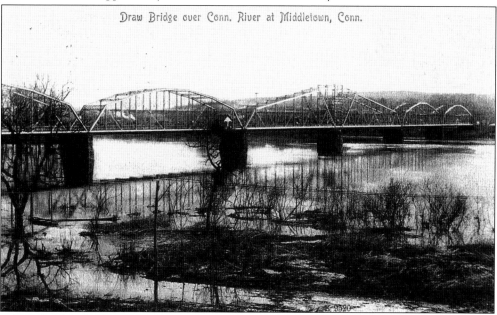

Draw Bridge over Conn. River at Middletown, Conn.

When the drawbridge pictured here was built in 1896, it allowed much easier access between Middletown and Portland than had been afforded by ferryboats. It was 1,300 feet long and had a 450-foot draw operated by electrical power, which at that time was the longest turnpike draw in the world. It opened to allow 200 feet of open river on each side.

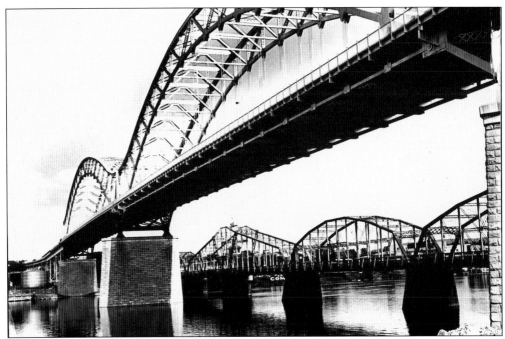

This 1938 photograph shows the closeness of the new Middletown–Portland Bridge of 1938 to its predecessor, the 1896 bridge. When the earlier bridge was first constructed, it was used by pedestrians and horses from 6:00 a.m. to 12:00 a.m. Between midnight and 6:00 a.m., it was left open for river traffic. The height of the new bridge allowed both land and river traffic nonstop passage.

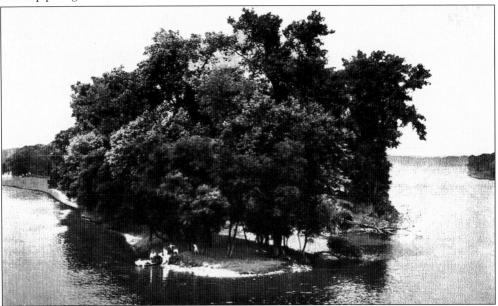

This 1914 postcard shows Willow Island. As the largest island in the Middletown stretch of the river, it lies just north of the highway bridge connecting Middletown and Portland. In the late 1800s, there was a footbridge from Middletown to the island, which contained a park at that time. A tip of the Portland quarry is visible on the right side of this photograph.

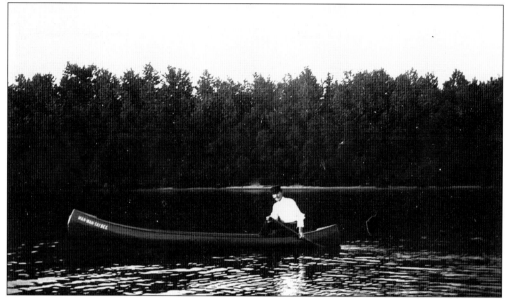

A canoe is passing Willow Island in 1894. Today canoeists are about the only people who set foot on the island, now commonly known as Wilcox Island. In 1897, Middletown's Mattabesett Canoe Club refurbished its clubhouse at the bottom of College Street, installing city water, electric lights, and an upright piano. At the time, it was storing 23 canoes for its 60 members.

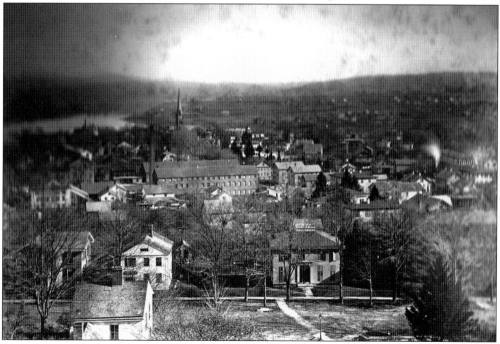

This photograph views the river and the south part of Middletown from the Wesleyan University campus. In the foreground is a section of High Street between William Street and Church Street. This is a typical view that future president Woodrow Wilson would have seen when he was professor of political economy for two years at Wesleyan University. He lived at 106 High Street from 1888 to 1890.

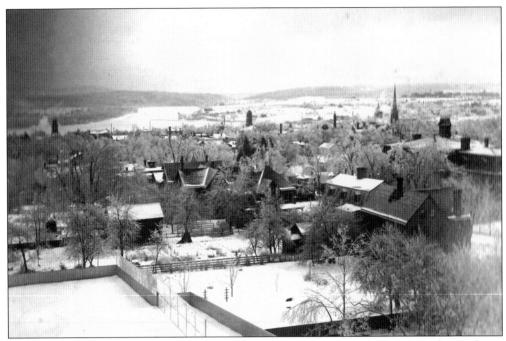

The snow scene in this photograph shows the bend in the Connecticut River from the Wesleyan University campus. The campus sits on the highest hill in downtown Middletown, up to 156 feet above sea level.

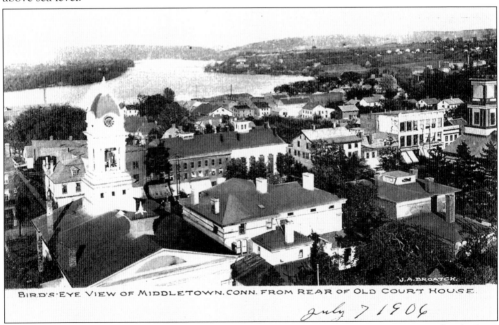

BIRD'S·EYE VIEW OF MIDDLETOWN. CONN. FROM REAR OF OLD COURT HOUSE.

J.A.BROATCH.

July 7 1906

This 1906 view looks east to the great bend of the Connecticut River. Water depth from Middletown north to Hartford was significantly less than the depth between the mouth of the river at Old Saybrook to Middletown. This prevented large trading vessels from moving beyond Middletown, thus making this town the most important port on the river. In the late 1700s and early 1800s, Middletown was the leading Connecticut River town in the West Indies trade.

This marker in downtown's Mortimer Cemetery marks the grave of one of two young members of the Russell family. Nearby is the grave of Patience and William's daughter Ruth, who died in 1817. Children often died from unknown causes that now can be cured with modern medicine. Sad epitaphs on gravestones indicate many children died at birth or in infancy; many died from smallpox and yellow fever.

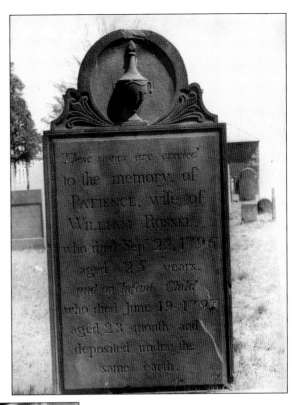

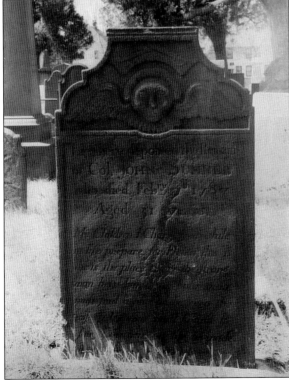

Revolutionary War veteran Col. John Sumner was buried in Mortimer Cemetery, several years after the war ended. His widow, Elizabeth, who died in 1825, lived to age 85. Middletown was known for its support of the colonists' cause. Many young men joined the armed service, while old men formed a home guard and women planted and harvested crops.

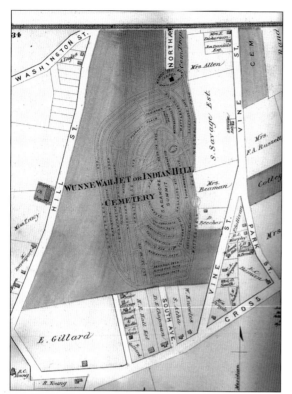

The area of Vine and Cross Streets on the lower right corner of this map was home to Middletown's African Americans in the 19th century. African American Leverett Beman, a member of an influential family active in the abolition movement, was instrumental in developing this area as an African American community. African American presence in Middletown goes back a long way; after Native Americans, African American and English families were the first to settle here.

Situated on the location of a 17th-century Native American stronghold, Indian Hill Cemetery is the final resting place for some of Middletown's most illustrious citizens, including governors, congressmen, and Congressional Medal of Honor recipients. Some of the nationally renowned people buried here are Civil War Gen. Joseph K. F. Mansfield, U.S. Postmaster General Samuel D. Hubbard, journalist Stewart Alsop, and Hollywood songwriter Allie Wrubel. The Gothic Revival chapel pictured here in 1888 was built in 1867 by Samuel Russell's widow, Frances Russell, who also founded the Russell Library.

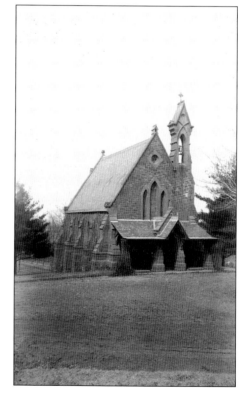

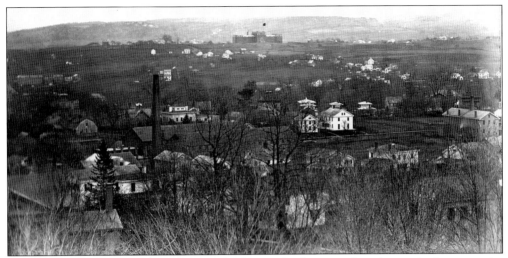

This photograph taken from High Street displays in the foreground residences, in the center the Goodyear Rubber Company, and to the right the Middletown Plate Company. In the background, the presence of the Connecticut Hospital for the Insane dominates the hilltop. The hospital was founded in 1867 and exists today as the Connecticut Valley Hospital.

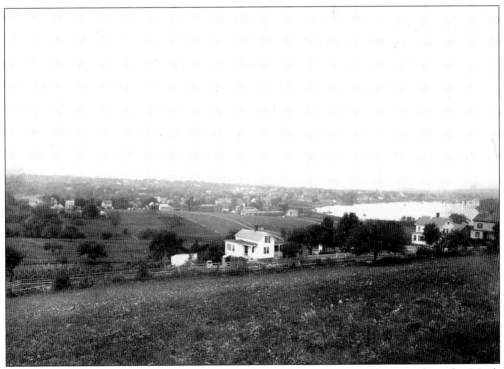

This view from the south part of Middletown shows the Connecticut River to the right. Much of the land outside of the city was devoted to farming. By the mid-1800s, most forest trees had been cleared from all but the borders of lots. Land clearing had such an effect on wildlife that the 1903 sighting of two deer by a traveler in south Middletown was reported in a major Hartford newspaper.

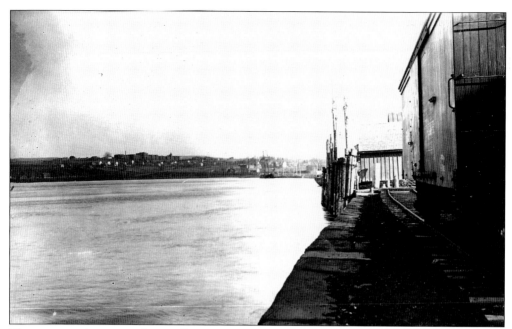

The two most important forms of business transportation for the first 250 years of Middletown's existence are seen in this photograph. A train car is pulled as close to the river as possible to allow goods to be transferred to and from ships. In the background, the huge Connecticut Hospital for the Insane sits on a hill in the most southeastern section of the Middletown.

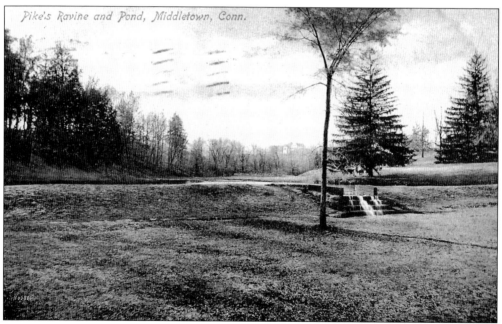

This peaceful scene of Pike's Ravine and Pond is a perfect example of the areas of Middletown that lay to the south and west of the city center. Prior to automobiles, Middletown families that lived downtown took trolley lines out to the countryside for Sunday picnics and country strolls.

Two

BUILDINGS AND STREETS

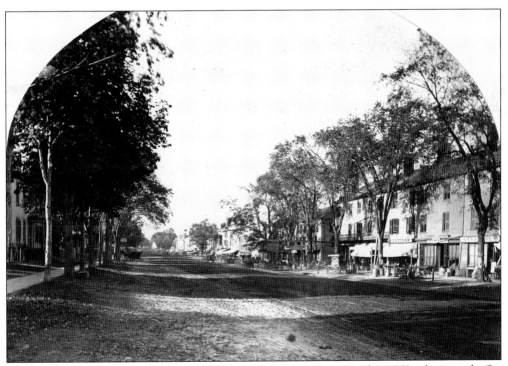

Many retail stores can be seen as one looks north up Main Street in this 1860s photograph. On the right side of the image are, from left to right, the Union Company, a livery stable, Parshley, C. E. Putnam, and Southmayd and Gardiner.

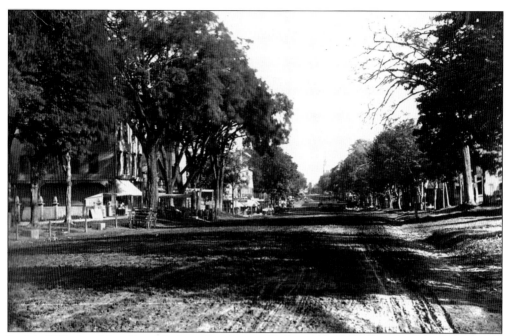

In this 1860 view, Main Street had an abundance of lush, verdant trees framing both sides, which supported Middletown's nickname "Forest City" although most of Middletown's dense forests disappeared. Smooth, level ground with sidewalks and storefronts like the one with barrels lined up are on the left, but note the unleveled ground on the right side of Main Street. In the distance is the South Congregational Church.

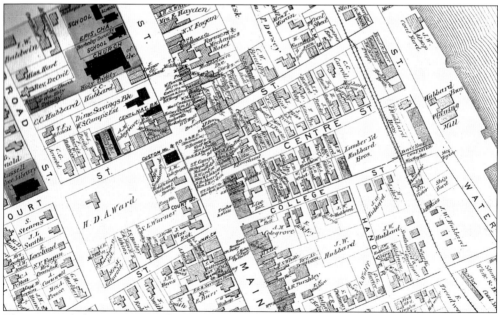

This map of downtown Middletown shows the buildings along Water Street before the construction of Route 9 effectively cut the city off from the river. It also marks the location of scores of buildings on and near the south part of Main Street that were demolished in the redevelopment efforts of the mid-1900s.

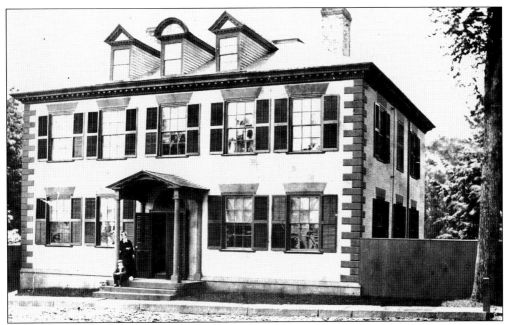

The DeKoven house, a dignified mansion of Georgian brick with a view of the Connecticut River, was originally built between 1791 and 1797 by Capt. Benjamin Williams, a wealthy West Indian trader. The house passed through the DeKoven family and was bequeathed to Col. Clarence Seymour Wadsworth (1872–1941). He used it as one of his homes until his mansion on Long Hill was completed, afterward using the DeKoven house as an office.

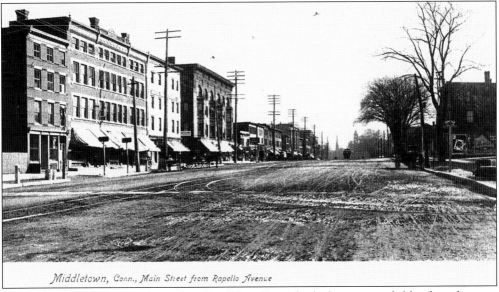

Middletown, Conn., Main Street from Rapello Avenue

Except for the telephone poles and trolley, Main Street looked pretty much like this when, on September 18, 1824, Revolutionary War leader Gen. Marquis de Lafayette, accompanied by his son, George Washington Lafayette, arrived in Middletown and traveled in a barouche pulled by four white horses. They rode up Washington Street, High Street, and Church Street. A meeting with Commodore Thomas Macdonough was followed by a reception at the Washington Hotel to the right of the trolley car in this picture.

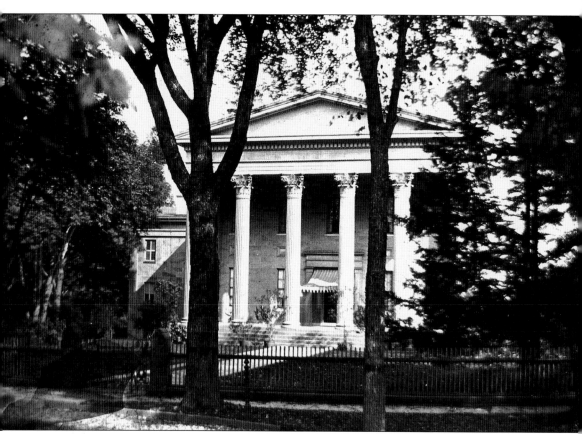

The Samuel Wadsworth Russell House, built in the Corinthian Greek Revival style, is a tribute to the success of this 19th-century adventurer, who founded the Russell Company and made his fortune from American–China trade. Russell's philanthropy was directed toward assisting those in need, especially in 1857 when local banks found themselves in serious financial difficulty. A story tells of the New Haven Eagle Bank's failure and how Russell's friend Samuel Hubbard salvaged its impressive Corinthian columns. He hired as many oxen and carts that could be found, carting the columns to the building site where they are now part of the distinguish front of the Russell House. The Russell House was built from 1827 to 1829, its original 22 rooms were enlarged to 42 rooms in 1860, and a north wing and modified front porch were added later. The Russell family lived here until 1936, after which the building was given to Wesleyan University. Many wedding parties have used the back of the Russell House and its landscape for their formal pictures. It is currently occupied by Wesleyan University's Honors College.

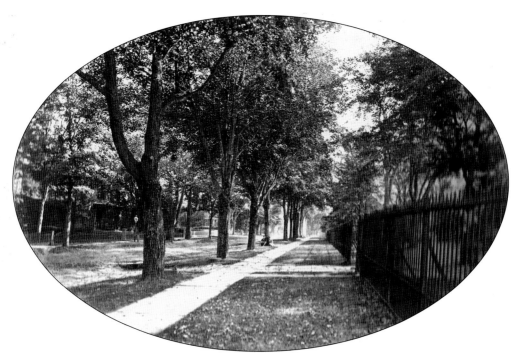

In this view of High Street looking south, two people are enjoying a break under the fourth tree back. It has been reported that the great British novelist Charles Dickens, on his 1867 trip to the United States, called High Street the most beautiful street in America.

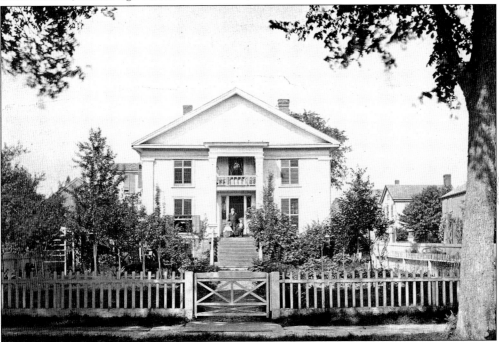

Samuel Converse stands on his porch with his wife, Sarah, and his daughter Carrie on a clear sunny day in 1880. This residence was on the corner of Liberty Street and Main Street in the city's north end.

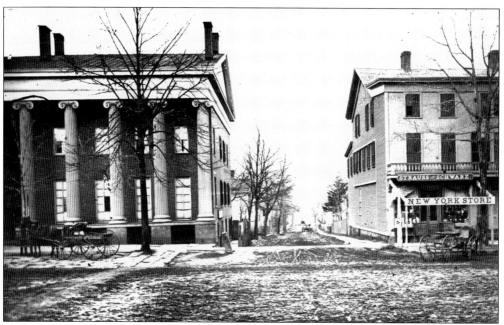

Looking down College Street from Main Street, the columned building on the left was the home of Connecticut governor Vincent Coffin. Moving to Middletown at age 28, Coffin served as mayor in 1872–1873, president of the Middlesex Mutual Assurance Company, state senator from 1886 to 1890, and Connecticut's governor from 1895 to 1897.

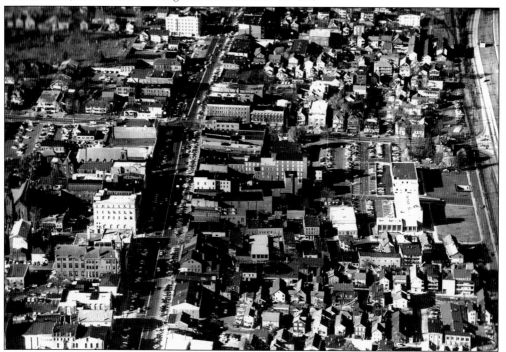

In this view of downtown, Main Street can be seen on the left heading north to the large Arrigoni Hotel. Most of the buildings in the lower right of this photograph were demolished during the redevelopment era to make room for Metro Square.

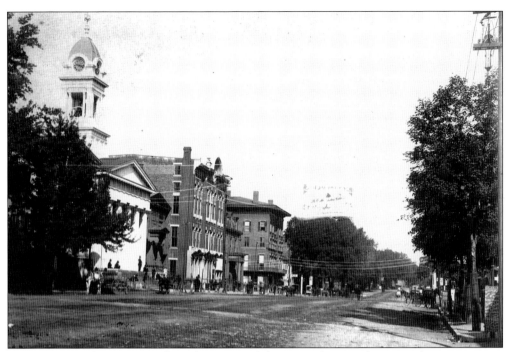

The McDonough House Hotel, in the center of this 1888 photograph, was under construction in 1851, opened in 1857, and was replaced by the Liberty Bank Building in 1928. The large white building to the left was the courthouse.

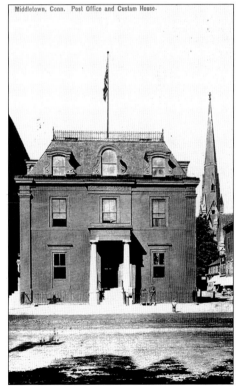

The Middletown Custom House located on Main Street had an entry porch with Doric columns. It replaced a wooden structure near the Connecticut River that collected taxes on imported goods. Completed in 1834, it was demolished to make room for a new post office building in 1916.

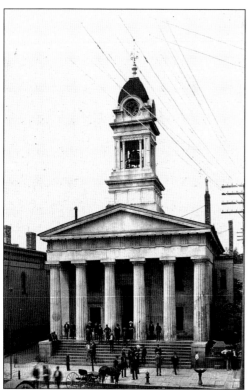

Replacing Middletown's original two-story wooden town hall in 1832, this second one was made of brick stucco and possessed a tall portico, 64 feet by 50 feet. Whereas the original courthouse's construction costs were paid in gallons of rum and molasses, this municipal building's construction cost was funded by the Town of Middletown, the City of Middletown, and the County of Middlesex. This town hall was razed 60 years later in 1892 and replaced by city hall with its distinctive clock tower. The latter, in turn, was demolished in 1961.

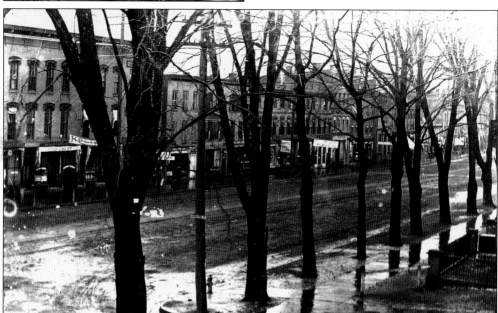

Middletown has one of the most attractive and widest main streets in the state; it is said that this is due to early settlers placing public buildings in the middle of the street to safeguard them from Native American attacks. Each household built houses on five-acre plots, east–west to Main Street. This 1908 photograph shows the wide street with stores on the left across Main Street selling "Stationary and Useful Holiday Goods" on a cold, rainy day.

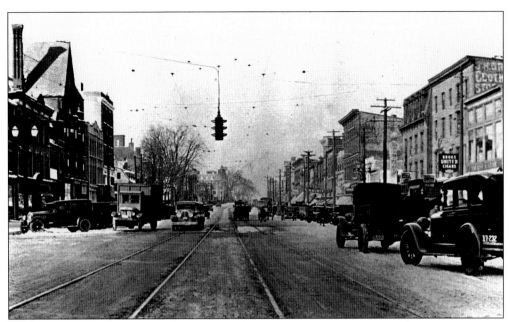

Double trolley tracks are visible in this *c.* 1925–1929 photograph, which illustrates that both trolleys and cars existed simultaneously in Middletown and were common modes of transportation during this time period. This section of Main Street between Court and Washington Streets has always attracted retail establishments. Some of the early stores seen on the east side of the street are, from right to left, a drug store, Bunce's, and Barton's.

In 1884, this bank block, which included Farmers' and Mechanics' Savings Bank, stood proudly alongside the customhouse on the right. It operated in Middletown for many years with the Bacon Law Offices and the Butler Insurance Company residing upstairs. In 1801, the Middletown National Bank was founded, with an initial raised capital of $75,000. It is visible on the left side of this photograph.

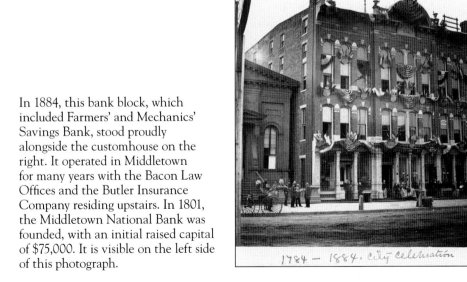

1784 – 1884. City Celebration

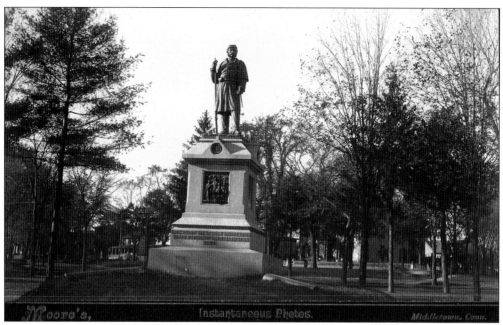

Sculptor Melzar Mosman's Civil War monument was set on Union Park (the South Green) in 1874. An eight-foot-high bronze Union soldier statue tops the monument in memory of the 110 Middletown soldiers and sailors who died for their country. The four cannons at the base of the monument were captured from the Confederacy.

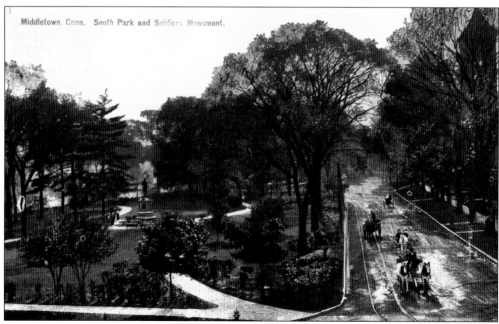

This 1910 postcard illustrates a busy corner at Union Park/South Park. Horse-drawn trolley tracks are seen along with horse-drawn buggies. Much in this area had changed from the early 19th century, when sailing ships traded Middletown goods like horses, cattle, sheep, beef, pork, flour, and lumber for molasses, sugar, rum, and salt.

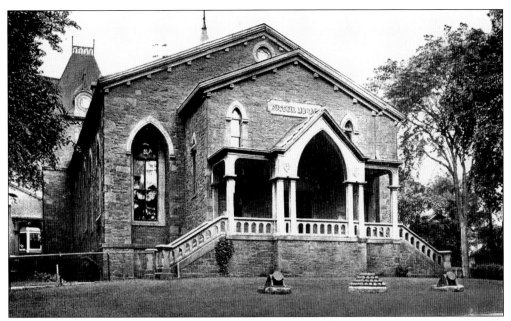

Today housing the Russell Library, this building was originally an Episcopal church. In 1873, Frances Russell, widow of China trader Samuel Russell, purchased the 39-year-old building from the Episcopal Church of the Holy Trinity. She had it remodeled in Roman Gothic style and in 1876 donated it to the inhabitants of Middletown for use as a public library. This c. 1922 photograph was taken when Edna Wilder was the head librarian. About eight years later, a children's room was added.

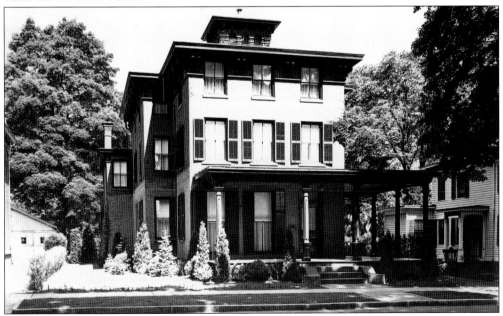

This ornate building was constructed around 1872 by Middletown chief of police John Wilcox. In 1881, it was bought by George Meech of Meech and Stoddard, who lived there until the 1930s. Purchased shortly thereafter by a Meech and Stoddard employee, it was transferred in 1973 to the Middlesex Memorial Hospital for use as office space.

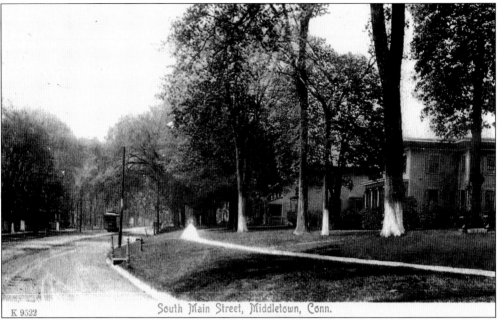

South Main Street, Middletown, Conn.

K 9322

This postcard of South Main Street was mailed in 1907, the same year that Antonio Pestritto was born in Middletown. Changing his name to Tony Pastor, he became the only saxophonist in Artie Shaw's band before starting his own big band in 1940. Considered the last of the big bands by many, Pastor's band continued until 1957. He died in 1969 and is buried in St. Sebastian's Cemetery.

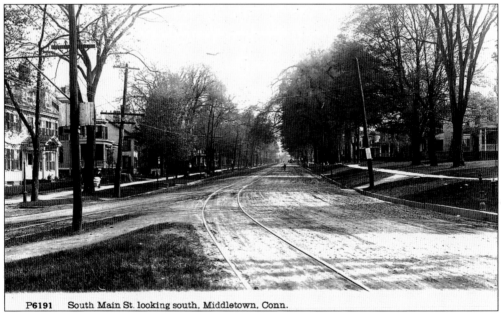

P6191   South Main St. looking south, Middletown, Conn.

With electricity, the city began to expand and grow as seen in this 1914 South Main Street photograph. Trolley tracks are seen heading south in the direction of the large factories in the Pameacha River area. Although trolleys and automobiles were common by this time, both sides of the street can be seen lined with horse hitching posts.

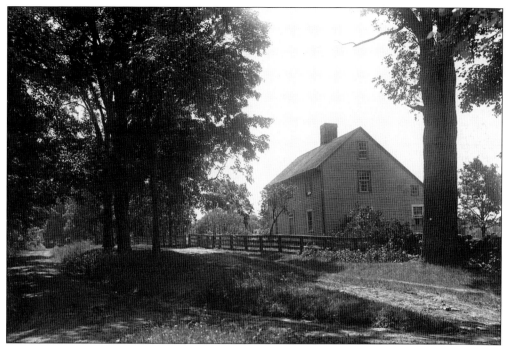

The Hubbard Homestead on Laurel Grove Road and Wadsworth Street was built in 1744. It was owned by Nehemiah Hubbard and the Hubbard family until 1916. Nehemiah Hubbard (1752–1837) was best known for furnishing supplies to the Colonial army during the American Revolution. In later years, he founded the city of Hubbard, Ohio, and returning to Connecticut, he became president of the Middletown Savings Bank.

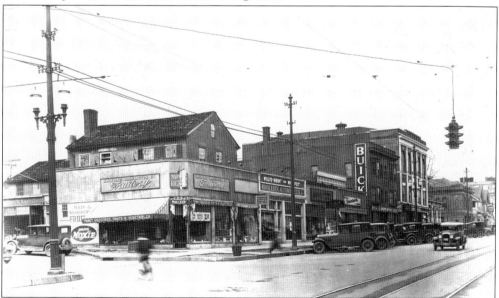

This c. 1929 photograph shows the Aristocrat Cleaning and Dyeing Company on Washington Street, Max Levin's Fruitery on the corner of Washington and Main Streets, and on Main Street, from left to right, the Middlesex Automobile Company, Blau's Electric Shop, Fountain's Flowers, F. L. Caulkin's Buick and Cadillac, John's Restaurant, and the Cho Mein Inn.

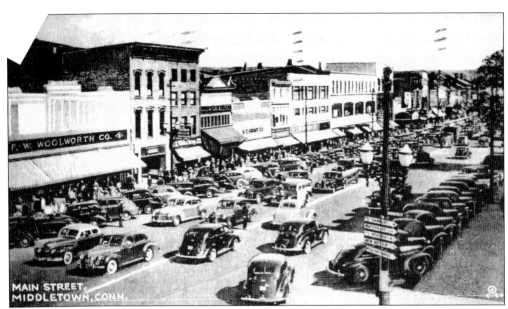

This postcard, mailed May 14, 1945, shows representatives of the major national department store chains F. W. Woolworth and W. T. Grant on Main Street. The road signs on the right point to Route 66 and list the westerly direction of Danbury, Waterbury, Meriden, New Britain, and the Wesleyan Campus. Today this major intersection on Main Street and Washington Street is still a busy location.

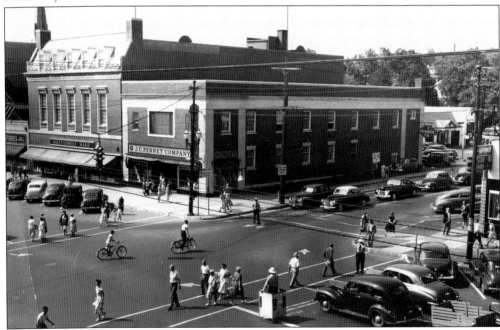

In this c. 1950 photograph, J. C. Penney's store is on the southwest corner of Washington and Main Streets. The exterior of these buildings changed little over the next half century while their occupants moved on. Today the J. C. Penney's site is currently empty, while the Montgomery Ward building houses Laser Tag. The traffic police box disappeared years ago but was a common sight during this time period. *I worked here full time when I turned 16*

This was 1941 *at .25 an hr.* *48 hrs a wk*
Interior decorator

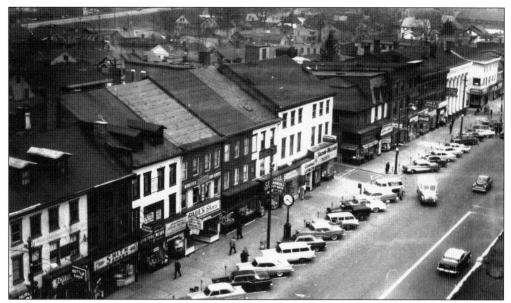

A rooftop view looking southeast on Main Street was captured on February 7, 1958, between Court Street and College Street. Although this photograph was taken to identify the needed restoration of this area, it captured the distinctive finned cars that were so common during this time. In the distance is Acheson Drive and the gas storage along the west bank of the Connecticut River.

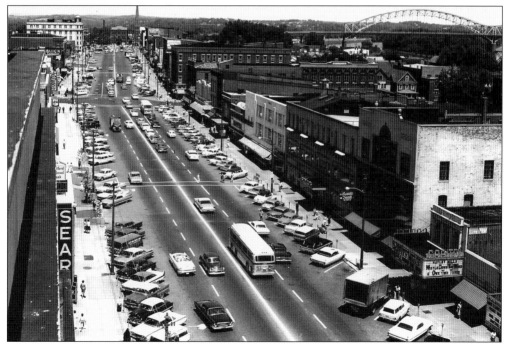

In 1962, the Arrigoni Hotel is at the upper left, St. John's steeple in the far distance at the north, and the Arrigoni Bridge is at the top right. The two movie theaters in the lower right are the Capital, showing a double feature of Hayley Mills in *Whistle Down the Wind* and *One, Two, Three*, while the Palace has the rerelease of the 23-year-old *Gone With the Wind*.

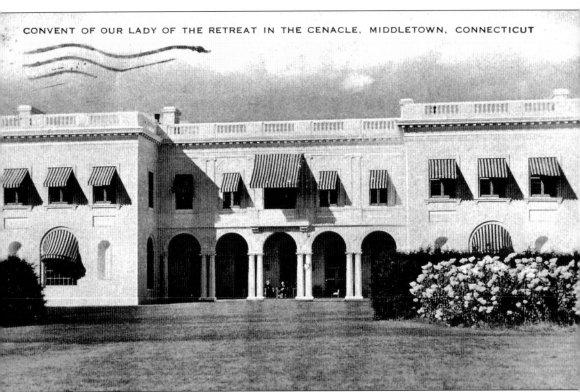

Katherine Hubbard Wadsworth's inherited land, with an additional 750 purchased acres, established the estate of Colonial Wadsworth, who used the Boston firm of the Olmsted Brothers to preserve and enhance the beauty of his natural surroundings while introducing a classic and formal site design as one approached his palatial summer home. The mansion, located at the western part of Middletown known as Long Hill, was designed by Hoppin and Koen and completed in 1917. In 1941, he bequeathed the estate of 267 acres to the State of Connecticut, allowing many residents enjoyment of Wadsworth Falls State Park, while the remainder of the estate was administered under the Rockfall Corporation, which he founded with his interests of conservation and forestry. In 1947, the estate was purchased for Our Lady of the Cenacle, a Roman Catholic order. Known locally as the "Cenacle," the convent provided meditation, shelter, religious instruction, and a serene environment to the community for almost 40 years and is seen in this postcard. From 1947 through 1986, the majority of the Long Hill estate was sold, becoming Mercy High School, Wilbert Snow School, and housing development sites. In 1994, Middletown purchased the bankrupt and vandalized ruin with its 103.5 acres, and restoration of the mansion and parklands took over two years with $5.8 million in funding. In 2000, Wadsworth Mansion was officially opened for community and private events, and its hiking trails and grounds are open to the public.

Three

EDUCATION

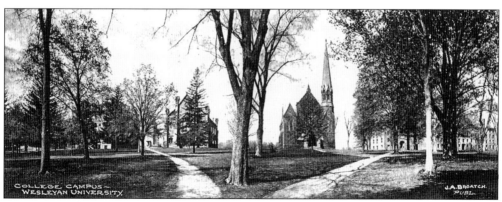

By 1889, Wesleyan had 23 faculty members, 231 students (with 1,500 graduates), and over $1.3 million in assets. Originally Middletown residents assisted a youthful Wesleyan by endowing $18,000. This 1908 photograph shows Wesleyan's College Row on High Street. Built using local brownstone, these buildings and the dates of their construction are, from left to right, Judd Hall (1872), the library (1869), the chapel (1871), and the observatory (1869).

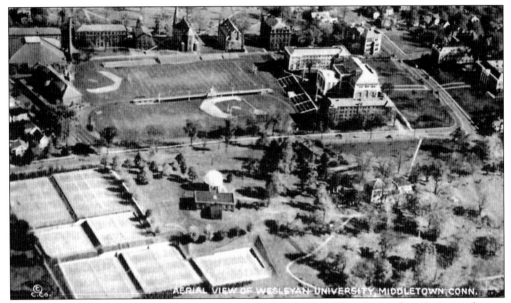

Wesleyan was founded under the auspices of the Methodist Church. In the 1944 aerial view seen above, one can make out the rear of the college row buildings across the top of the picture, forming the eastern border of Andrus Field. They are, from left to right, North College, South College, Memorial Chapel, the old library, and Judd Hall. The large building that occupies much of the upper right quadrant is Olin Library. Founded in 1831 as an all-male school, women were admitted in 1872. In 1912, it reverted back to an all-male school. It was not until 1968 that women students again gained admittance.

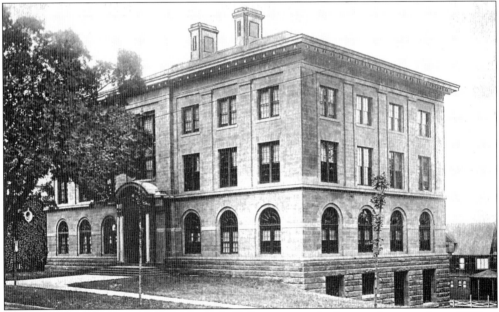

Built in 1904, Wesleyan University's Fisk Hall was named after its first president, Willbur Fisk. With a background as a Methodist preacher and an antislavery leader, he inspired the university community during its first years. Today Fisk Hall is the home of the Wesleyan's Office of International Studies, the coordinator of student study abroad programs.

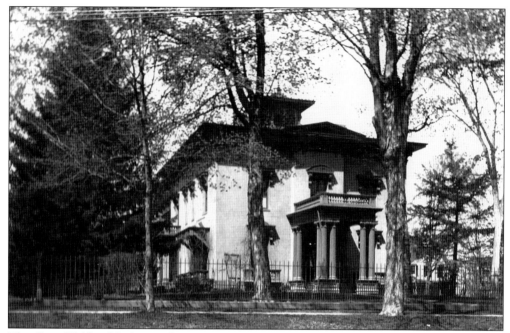

The Coite-Hubbard Italianate house, at Wyllis Avenue and High Street, was built in 1856 for Gabriel Coite, who became a state senator in 1860. In 1863, he sold the house to Jane Miles Hubbard, the widow of Samuel Hubbard. Samuel, a Middletown native, had manufacturing interests in town and was a lawyer, Connecticut representative to the 29th and 30th Congresses, and postmaster general of the United States under Pres. Millard Fillmore. Jane's heirs bequeathed the President's House to Wesleyan in 1904.

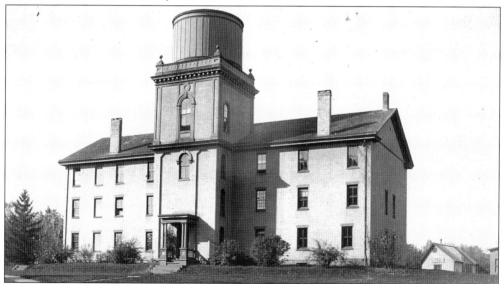

In 1839, Wesleyan University erected this building known as the "New Boarding House," where it was first used as a dormitory. In the fall of 1869, it was remodeled and a striking tower was added, which had one of Alvan Clark's popular refracting telescopes, thereafter becoming known as "Observatory Hall." Students once used this building for classes in mathematics. It was torn down in 1927.

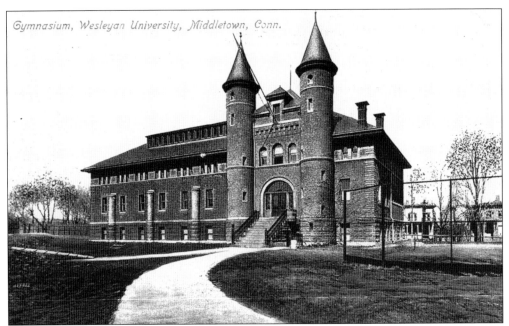

Imposing Romanesque towers front the Fayerweather Gymnasium around 1930. Designed by noted architect J. C. Cady, who also designed numerous buildings for Yale University and the south part of the American Museum of Natural History in New York City, Fayerweather Gymnasium was completed in 1894 at the north end of College Row. It was recently restored with its first floor now used for theater and dance space, while its second floor, Beckham Hall, is used for lectures.

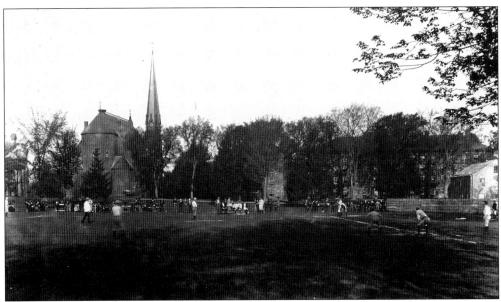

The spectators are tense on a sunny afternoon on May 11, 1889, which has Wesleyan's William H. Kidd at the bat in the 10th inning with a score of 7-7 at Andrus Field behind North College. It was one of the most controversial baseball games played that year.

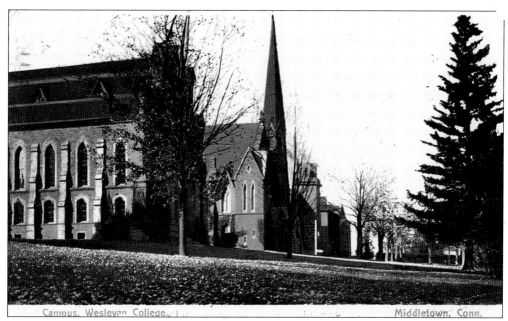

This early-20th-century photograph shows the buildings of Wesleyan's College Row on High Street. These buildings are, from left to right, Judd Hall, the library, the chapel, the observatory, and North College. Memorial Chapel honors 13 students and alumni who died during the Civil War. Rich Hall Library is now the Patricelli '92 Theater.

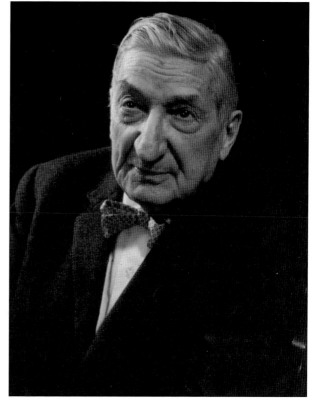

Charles Wilbert Snow was a respected professor at Wesleyan University from 1921 to 1952. A renaissance man, Wilbert Snow was known for his poetry, his friendship with Robert Frost and Carl Sandburg, his public service as Connecticut lieutenant governor and governor, and his role in the founding of the state's community college system. In 1954, Middletown's Snow Elementary School was named after him. (Courtesy Wesleyan University.)

41

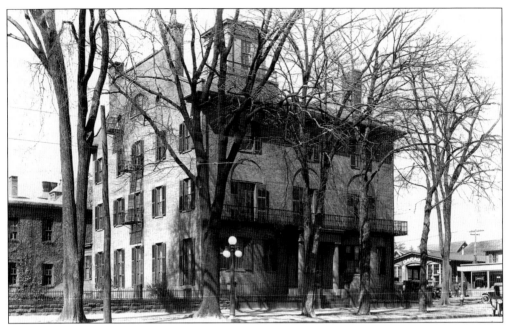

This brick building on the southwest corner of Main and Washington Streets was built in 1812 as the Washington Hotel. It later became the Berkley Divinity School. It was founded by Anglican Bishop John Williams, who was its dean for more than 40 years. The school moved to New Haven in 1928, and in 1971, it became affiliated with Yale Divinity School. The building pictured here was razed in 1928.

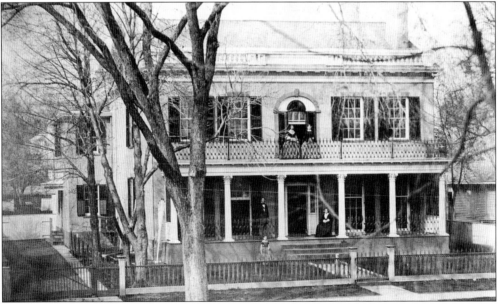

Daniel Chase's Preparatory School, at the north end of Main Street, educated 80 students from 1835 to 1870. The next occupant was Arthur W. Magill, owner of Middletown Manufacturing Company, who first used steam power in his woolen mill. Some of the other boardinghouses and hotels were the New York Hotel, Germania House, Hotel Mattabesett, Hotel Herbert, and Ideal Hotel.

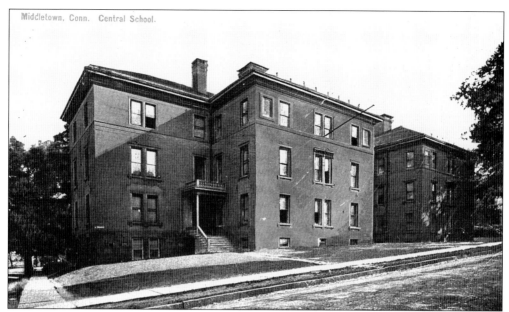

Middletown, Conn. Central School.

A new high school was considered in 1839 after deciding to consolidate four central districts. Temporarily, 200 students sat on homemade benches, attending classes in the Episcopal church's basement, which is now the Russell Library. Middletown High School, the first high school in Connecticut, was opened on College Street in 1840. After an addition in 1869, it was renamed Central School. When it burned in 1878, it was rebuilt after one term. This high school closed in 1895.

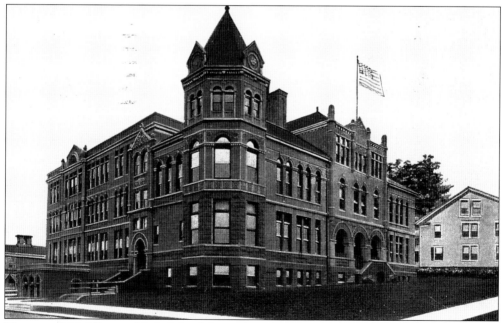

The second Middletown High School, located on Court and Pearl Streets opened in 1895 and was used until 1972, when a new high school was opened near Newfield Street on what was then called Tiger Lane. The brick and brownstone high school, seen in this c. 1928 picture, was later renovated for use as senior citizens' housing.

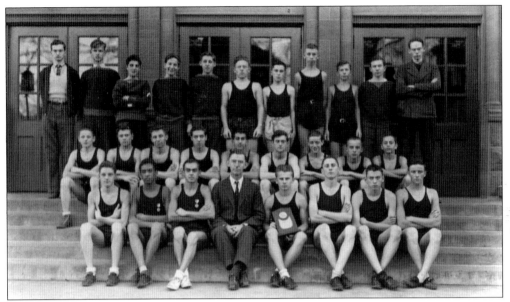

Middletown High School cross country team members in 1937–1938 are, from left to right, (first row) V. Larson, F. Warmsley, Romolo "Ron" Cannemella, Carlyle G. Hoyt (coach), Walter Kowal (class of 1938 team captain), W. Powers, Arthur Daniels, and John Cronley; (second row) T. Milinka, R. Kogan, Salvatore Alessi, F. Marchese, Salvatore Crescimanno, Raymond Rafferty, B. Quirk, S. Kowal, and T. Scionti; (third row) Charles Palmer (class of 1938 team manager), R. Kardas, ? Damiata, A. Fain, L. Curtis, Edward Knecht, J. Coughlin, F. Kornetta, L. Cyprano, A. Anderson, and R. Bruce.

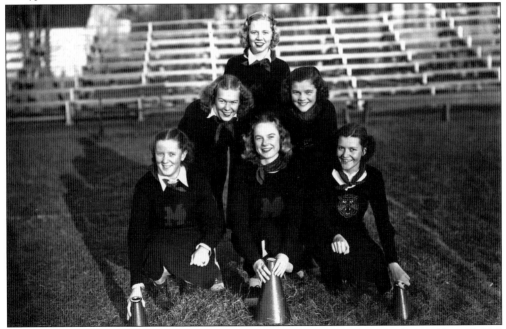

Middletown High School's 1938 cheerleaders from left to right are (first row) Geraldine "Jiddy" Larson, lead cheerleader Arline Johnson, and Catherine Cox; (second row) Elsie Johnson and Marjorie Herrmann; (third row) Juwil Child.

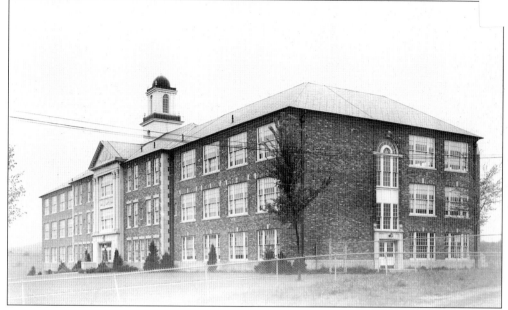

Woodrow Wilson High School on Hunting Hill Avenue is seen in this 1936 photograph. In 1956, it was moved into a newly constructed building across the street. It had a competitive rivalry with Middletown High until they were consolidated in 1984.

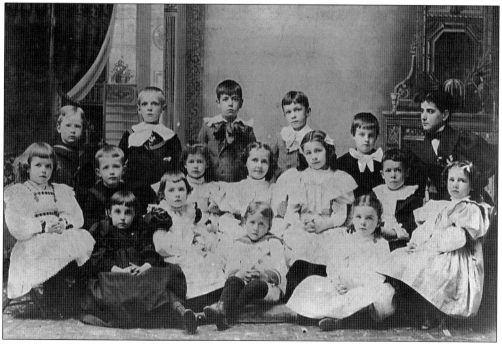

Miss Annie Watrous's kindergarten class from May 1895 includes, from left to right, (first row) two unidentified, Dudley Butler, and Faith Bonfoey; (second row) Marguerite Ward, Leroy Ward, Florence Smith, Hortense Fairman, Dorothea Pearse, Carlton Caukins, and Ruth Fairman; (third row) possibly Theodore Greene, Dick Northrop, Bob Pike, possibly Roger Bacon, Kenneth MacDougal, and Watrous (teacher).

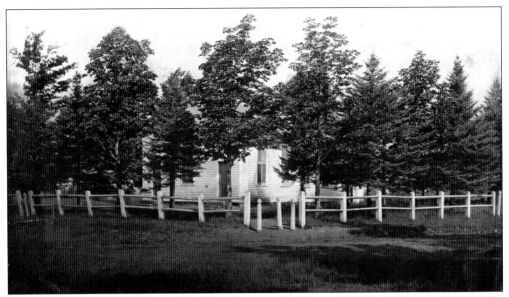

Many children were taught at this first district schoolhouse in Westfield around 1890. Its original site is where the Westfield Fire House now stands. During the 19th century, there were four district schools in the Westfield section of Middletown until about 1910, when the superintendent consolidated these schools into one. Before attending Middletown High School, outlying students would have to show their mastery of their primary education by taking an entrance exam if they wanted admittance. The trolley assisted students in getting to school until about 1930, when it was discontinued. Students had to find their own way into the center of town for additional schooling until after World War II, when bus service was made available to them.

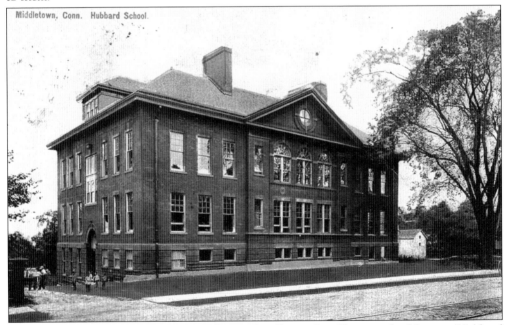

Education was important to many settlers and still is today. Photographed here is Hubbard School, located on Loveland Street.

Four

CHURCHES AND
ORGANIZATIONS

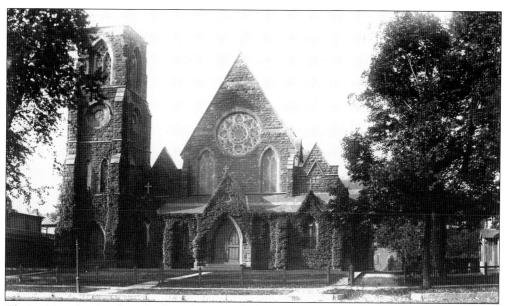

Christ Church, the first Anglican/Episcopal church in Middletown, was built in 1755 and was used until 1834. The parish then erected a new church at the corner of Broad and Court Streets. That building is now the south section of the Russell Library. When the building was sold, the parish built the present Gothic Revival church of local brownstone on Main Street. Completed in 1874, it is pictured here in an 1886 photograph. Benefactor Martha Starr required as a condition of her gift that it be renamed the Church of the Holy Trinity.

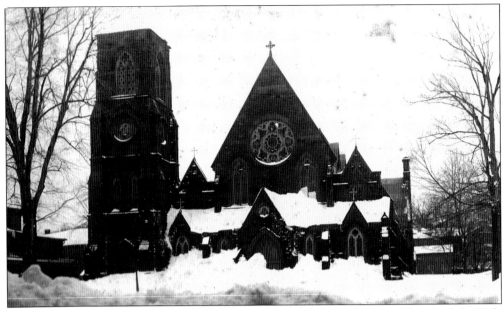

Five years after this March 1887 photograph, Dr. Edward Acheson became Church of the Holy Trinity's rector. His son, Dean, secretary of state under Pres. Harry Truman, recalled in 1949, "Father knew everybody in town—the harness maker, the policeman, the garbage collector . . . A walk up Main Street used to be an ordeal. Father said, 'Now come on, Dean, we're going down to the post office.' Well, I knew that was a morning shot to hell."

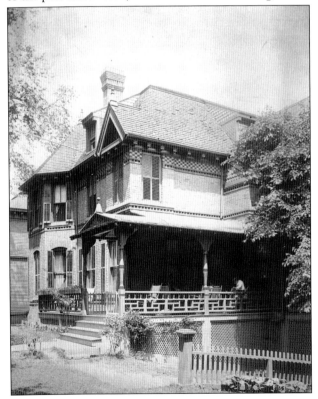

Located on Broad Street, this building served as the old rectory of the Church of the Holy Trinity. The Episcopal parish was originally organized by 16 families in the 1740s when the state Congregational church waned in its dominance. The Episcopal Society formed Christ Church in 1750, and it was later renamed Church of the Holy Trinity. Dr. Edward Acheson served as rector of Church of the Holy Trinity until 1915, eventually becoming the Episcopal bishop of Connecticut.

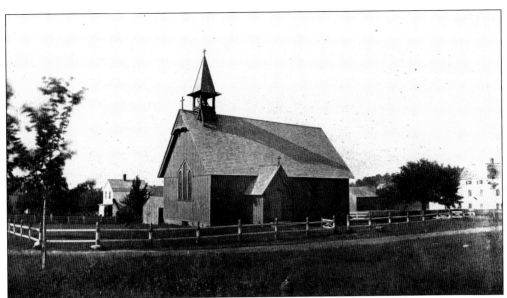

Along with Christ Church in the South Farms area of Middletown and St. Andrews on Warwick Street, All Saints Church on Staddle Hill, shown in this early photograph, was founded as a mission of downtown's Church of the Holy Trinity. This All Saints Church building eventually became Staddle Hill School. In 1935, the other three elementary schools were Farm Hill, Durant School, and Long Hill School.

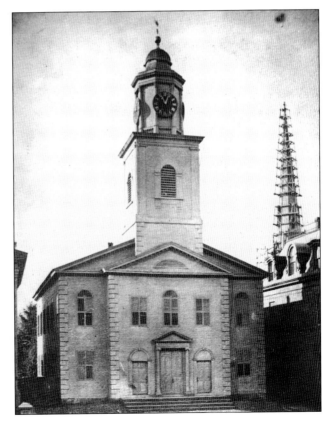

At a glance, the townspeople could view the prominent clock displayed on the congregation meetinghouse. While in the background, Middletown residents viewed the steeple of the First Church of Christ, which was being built during 1873. Its dedication was on May 1, 1873, and it was the fifth building to have housed this church.

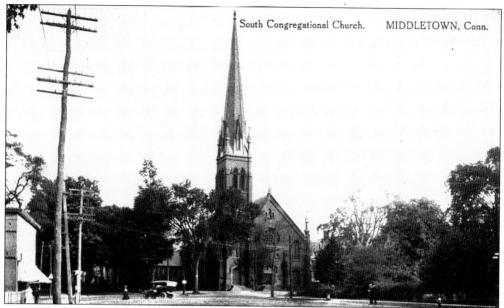

South Congregational Church.   MIDDLETOWN, Conn.

In the 1750s, Congregationalists from Wethersfield founded South Congregational Church in an effort to find freedom from the official church of the colony. In 1830, they built the first church at its present location at Main and Pleasant Streets. This was replaced in 1867 by the present church, pictured here in a 1916 postcard. South Congregational Church established the town's first Sunday school in 1828 and was active in the antislavery movement, and for over a century, its members have performed volunteer work at the Connecticut Valley Hospital.

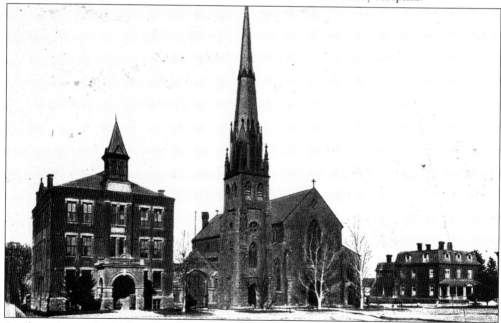

At the other end of Main Street from South Congregational Church is St. John's Roman Catholic Church. This photograph, taken in 1907, shows the church school building on the left and the rectory on the right. On this site, Irish immigrants built the first permanent Catholic church in Middletown in 1844. After its destruction from fire, it was rebuilt in 1889.

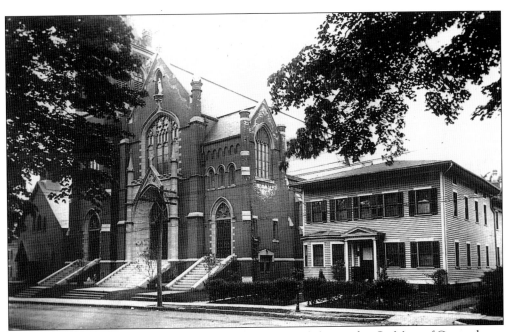

Fronting on Hubbard Street, the small building on the far left served as St. Mary of Czestochowa Church for several years (around 1905 to around 1907), thereafter becoming St. Mary's School. St. Mary's beautiful stained-glass church in the center was completed in 1912 and was destroyed by fire in 1980. It was rebuilt behind the church pictured here. The building on the right served as the original convent until its demolition in 1963. (Courtesy Anne Toczko Nowakowski.)

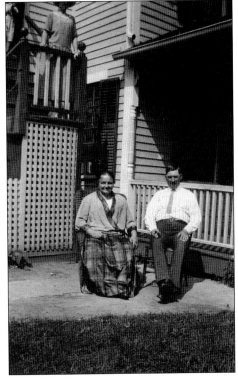

Lifetime parishioners of St. Mary of Czestochowa Church, John and Katherine Wiernasz sit outside their home on Goodyear Avenue in about 1915, while their daughter Helen stands above. John was one of the founders of the parish in 1903 and was the first person of Polish descent to serve as a police officer in Middletown. (Courtesy Anne Toczko Nowakowski.)

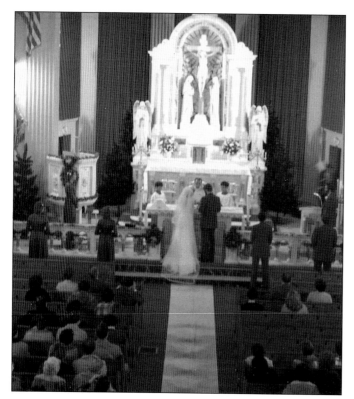

St. Sebastian's Church on Washington Street was completed in 1931 by Middletown's Italian community. Many parishioners contributed their skills as masons, stone carvers, and other occupations to the construction of the church. The Middletown church was modeled after a church with the same name in Melilli, Sicily, the ancestral home of most of Middletown's Italians. The main altar of St. Sebastian's Church appears in this photograph.

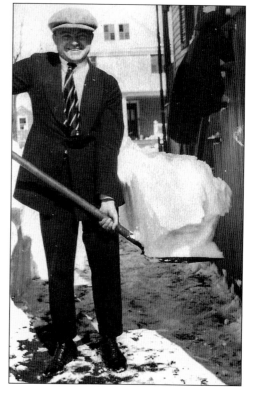

St. Sebastian's Church parishioner Joseph Settipane is seen here shoveling snow at his home on Cherry Street around 1930. A tiny street near the Connecticut River, Cherry Street was the location of Revolutionary War Gen. Comfort Sage's home. A story has been handed down that in 1780 Sage's wife, Sarah, hid Benedict Arnold's two young sons from a Middletown mob that rioted through the streets and hung the traitor in effigy when they learned of his treason.

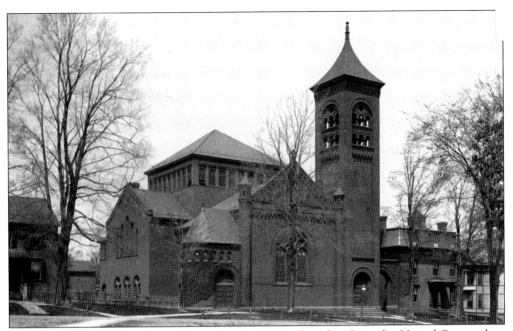

The Methodist Episcopal Church was the first Methodist church in the United States when it split with the Anglicans in 1784. The early church was known for its opposition to slavery. It has since become part of today's United Methodist Church. This c. 1910 picture shows the Methodist Episcopal Church in Middletown.

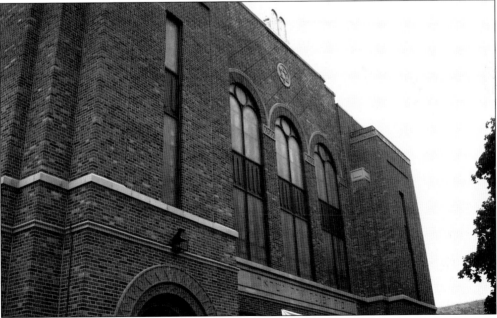

Most Jewish immigrants from Europe settled in Portland until the Middletown congregation was incorporated in 1905. They then met in private homes, later purchasing a two-family house on Union Street. In 1929, Congregation Adath Israel's synagogue was dedicated. Pictured in this photograph with its triple-arched stained-glass window, it is located on the northwest corner of Middletown's South Green.

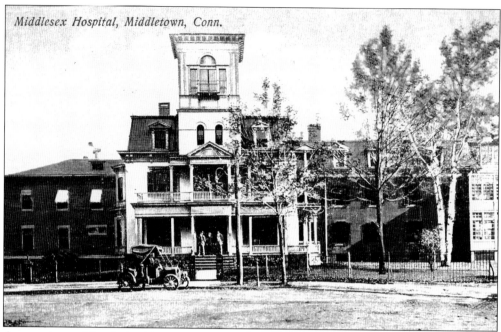

A committee of local physicians was organized in 1895 to build a hospital in Middletown. In 1903, the land on Crescent Street along with the homestead of Col. Herbert L. Camp and his sister, Mrs. E. Hershey Smith, provided the hospital with a new home. It is photographed here around 1906. A three-year training school for nurses was established in 1908. In 1945, one-day patient care cost less than $7.

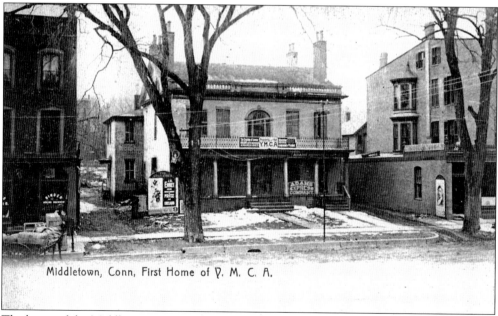

The home of the Middletown YMCA is pictured in this c. 1907 postcard. In the early years, the YMCA reading room was open about seven hours per day, and lecture courses were sponsored. The building seen here on Main Street was occupied by the YMCA from 1892 to 1927. Subsequently a new building was constructed on the corner of Union and Crescent Streets.

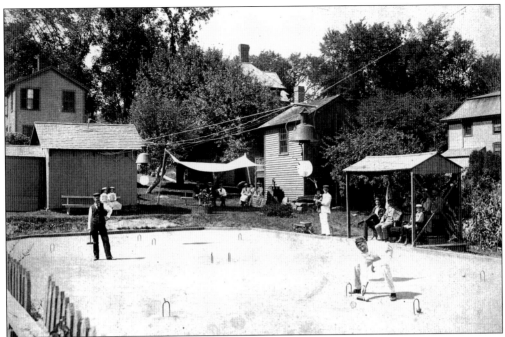

A croquet game is taking place at the Butler house on High Street in 1896. Very popular in English-speaking countries in the 19th century, the game was to a large extent overtaken by tennis, with many croquet lawns converted into tennis courts.

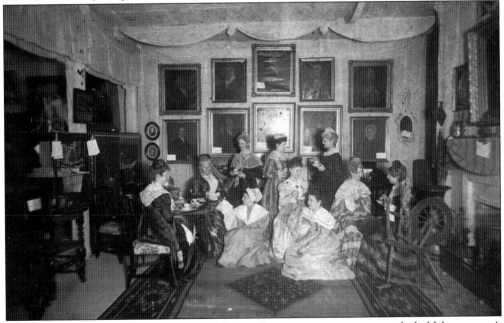

Events like this 1893 reenactment of a Colonial tea party were commonly held by women's historical associations during the late 1800s. Attending this c. 1890s event is Grace Hubbard Bunce prior to her marriage to Capt. William Paulding in 1896. At the present time, the Middlesex County Historical Society continues to hold annual events, like a Victorian tea, which serves a dual purpose of pleasure and raising funds.

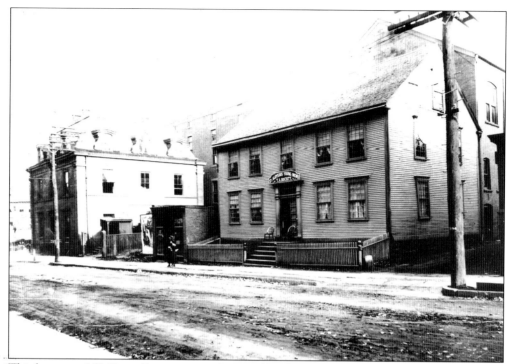

This house on 159 Court Street was used in 1915 by the St. Aloysius Young Men's Temperance Society, which was very popular at that time because it served a social and political movement. Before this location, it met at North Congregational Church and other churches in the area.

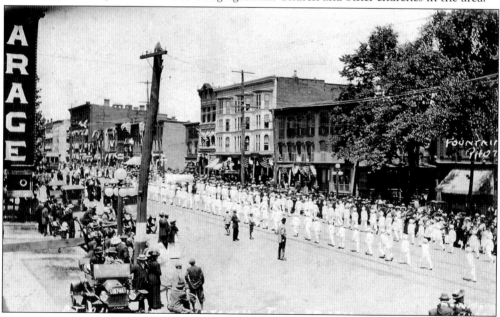

This photograph is of the Catholic Total Abstinence Union Parade in Middletown on June 30, 1914. This organization, founded as a federation of Roman Catholic temperance groups, had its national headquarters in Hartford. There is mention of an active Middletown Temperance Convention in 1850 with speeches, reports, parades, and the singing of temperance songs.

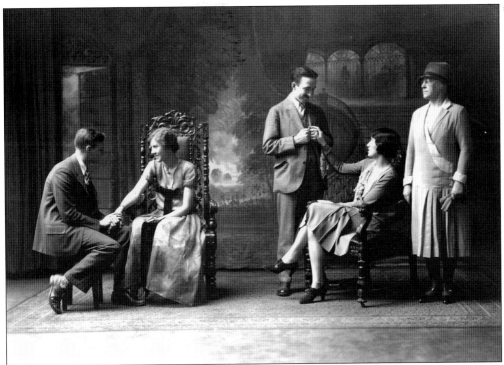

The first production of the Little Theatre Guild's first season 1927–1928 was *Mr. Pim Passes By*. The three-act comedy, set in an English country home, was written by Winnie the Pooh creator, A. A. Milne. Directed by F. C. Strickland, Wesleyan University's drama coach, the cast included female lead Edith Sage, along with Polly Wells, Marguerite Losey, Edward Murtfeldt, Alice Sitterly, and Dr. Harold Davis.

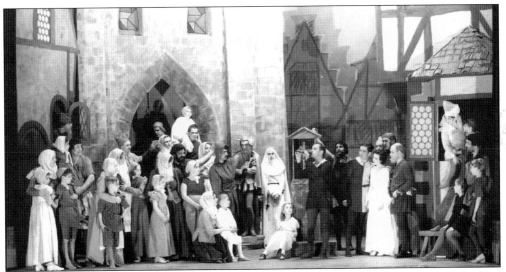

The Little Theatre Guild produced *The Piper*, Josephine Preston Peabody's version of the *Pied Piper of Hamelin*. The verse drama was first published in 1909 and produced on the New York and London stages. Little Theatre Guild performances were on May 10 and 11, 1932, in the Patricelli '92 Theater at Wesleyan's Rich Hall.

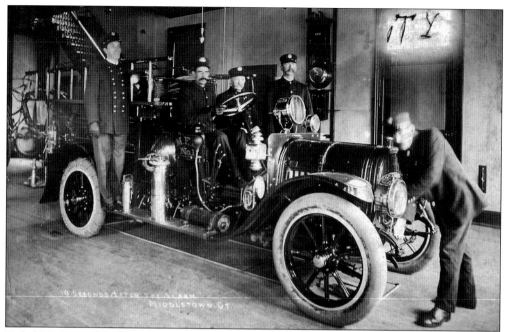

Titled "10 Seconds After This Alarm," this photograph depicts Middletown Fire Department's ladder truck No. 1 in the early 20th century. Middletown's first fire company was organized in 1803, and the law stated that every building had "to keep in constant state of readiness and repair one good leather bucket containing not less than 2 gallons."

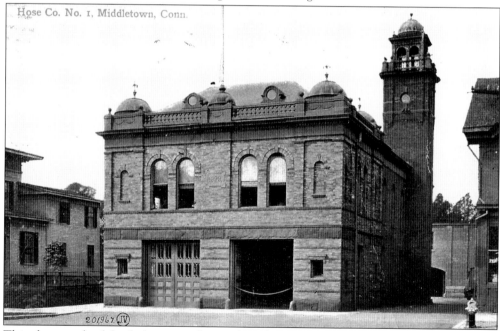

This photograph of the firehouse on the north end of Main Street was taken in 1911. Between 1910 and 1912, its Pope-Hartford auto chemical truck answered 139 fire alarms. During these two years, about $100 was spent on truck expenses while $1,900 was needed to maintain the horses for older vehicles.

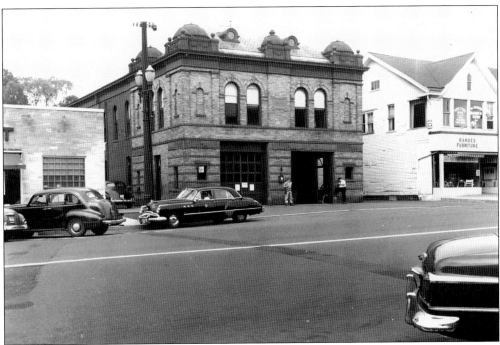

This 1952 photograph of the Main Street Firehouse taken during an air raid drill has a rifle-bearing guard standing in front. During weekday fire drills, loud, long sirens signaled schoolchildren to head to the basements. For decades, residents heard this alarm sounding every first Saturday of the month, and it also interrupted their radio broadcasts. Air Raid Shelters were distinctly marked for the safety of citizens and had emergency provisions within them.

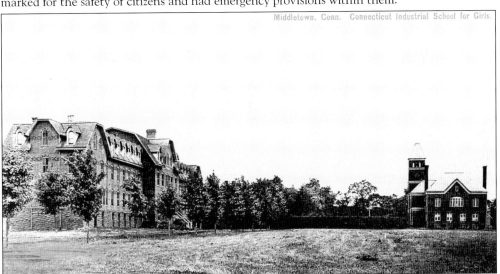

The private charity of Connecticut Industrial School for Girls, seen in this c. 1911 postcard, was founded in 1868. When land in Middletown was donated in 1870, it provided a new home for delinquent girls aged 8 to 16. Caroline Penniman, its first female superintendent, used a novel approach, with girls earning privileges and freedoms as rewards. Also known as Long Lane Farm (1921) and Long Lane School (1943), the land and buildings were purchased by Wesleyan University for $15 million in 1999.

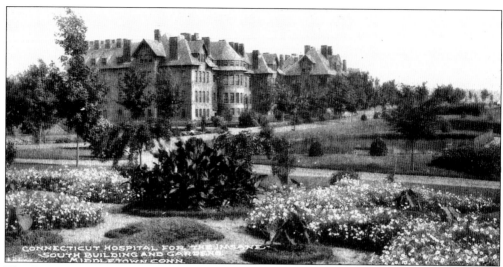

The Connecticut Hospital for the Insane opened in 1868. The institution sat atop high ground downriver from the center of town with impressive views of the Connecticut River. Many original buildings were built with brownstone, while the newer ones used brick. It had main, middle, and south hospitals, an annex, and five cottages landscaped with fountains, bright flowers, and a large expanse of lawns and trees.

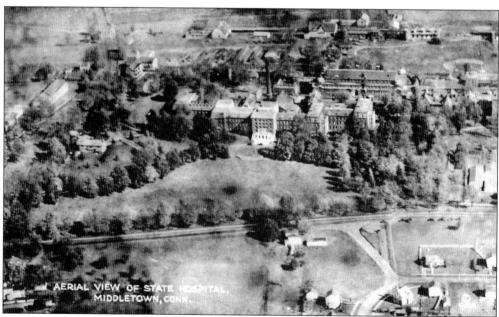

This 1946 aerial view of the Connecticut State Hospital shows a number of large, impressive buildings. Back in 1887, patients numbered about 1,300. By 1900, about 2,000 patients resided at the hospital. In 1953, the new state Department of Mental Health was charged with the administration of the hospital. Since 1961, it has been known as the Connecticut Valley Hospital or CVH.

Five

PEOPLE

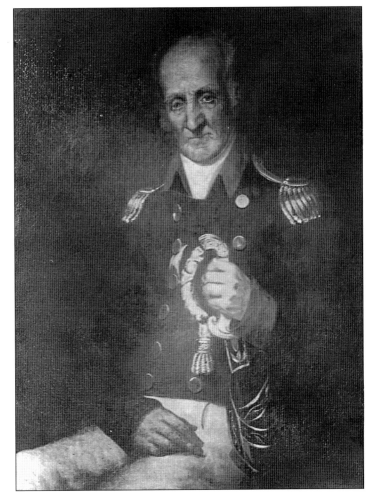

The painting in this photograph of Revolutionary War hero Col. Return Jonathan Meigs was presented to the Middlesex County Historical Society on September 9, 1907. Born in Middletown in 1740, Meigs was captured during the invasion of Quebec and later exchanged and promoted to the rank of colonel. In 1777, he commanded a regiment that surprised the British force at Sag Harbor, Long Island, destroyed 12 vessels, and captured almost 100 men without a single American casualty. At the age of 48, he moved from Middletown to Ohio, becoming an agent to the Cherokees.

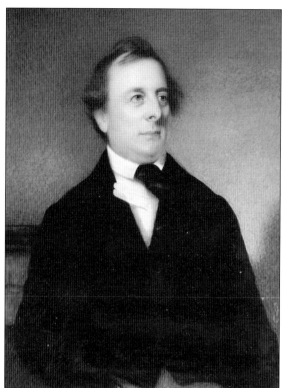

Born in Middletown in 1799, Samuel Dickinson Hubbard graduated from Yale College in 1819, worked as a lawyer and a businessman, was elected to Congress, and in 1852, was appointed to fill the position of postmaster general of the United States in Pres. Millard Fillmore's cabinet. A century later, another Middletown native, Dean Acheson, would serve in Pres. Harry Truman's cabinet as secretary of state.

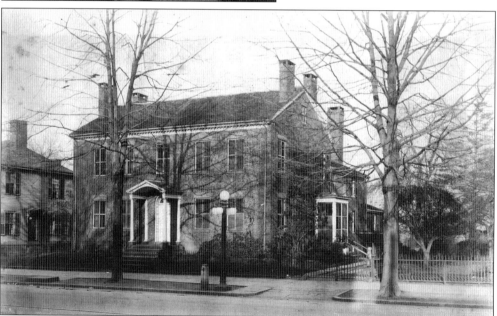

The Federal-style Mansfield House was built for Samuel Mather in 1810. In 1854, it was given to his daughter, Louisa Maria, who had married U.S. Army Capt. Joseph Mansfield in 1838. Except for a five-year period when they lived in Massachusetts, this house was their official residence until Joseph's death in 1862. A Mansfield family descendant transferred ownership of the house to the Middlesex County Historical Society in 1959. It has been the society's home ever since.

Born in 1803, Gen. Joseph K. F. Mansfield served 20 years with the Corps of Engineers and was seriously wounded in the Mexican War. At the beginning of the Civil War, he was placed in charge of the defense of Washington, D.C. On September 17, 1862, as a commander at the Battle of Antietam, Mansfield was mortally wounded while personally leading a brigade into battle on horseback. His body was returned to Middletown for burial.

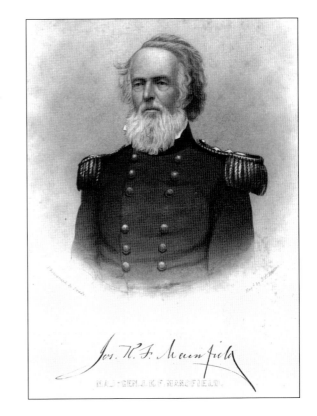

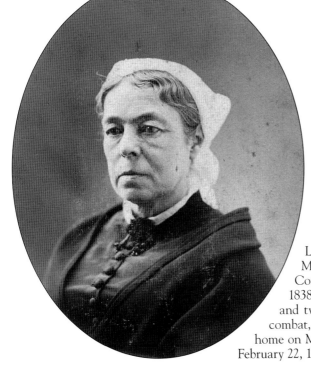

Louisa Mather married Joseph Mansfield, a U.S. Army captain in the Corps of Engineers, on September 25, 1838. They had five children, three sons and two daughters. After Joseph's death in combat, Louisa continued to live at the family home on Main Street, Middletown. She died on February 22, 1880, at age 71.

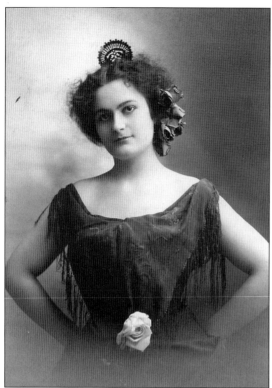

Gen. Joseph Mansfield's granddaughter Louise is pictured here in the late 1800s. Her father, Henry Livingston Mansfield, the fourth-born child of Joseph and Louisa Mansfield, married Adeline Carter in 1866. Living on Broad Street, in the building later occupied by the Middletown District Nurse Association, they had two daughters, Louise and Ellie. Ellie passed away in 1940, and Louise died in 1957.

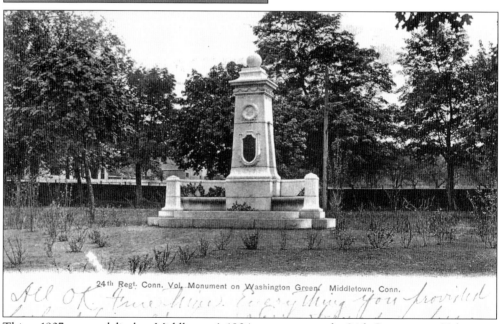

This c. 1907 postcard displays Middletown's 1904 monument to the 24th Connecticut Volunteers in the Civil War. The monument lists the names of the 13 Middletown men who were killed in action, the 8 men who died from their wounds, and the 53 men who died of other causes. Some 20 of Middletown's African American men, of a total population of only 173 people, served in the 29th Volunteer Infantry Regiment.

William Van Deursen was a first sergeant in Company F in the 24th Connecticut Infantry from September 3, 1862, to September 30, 1863. Born in Middletown, Van Deursen was wounded at the Battle of Port Hudson. After the Civil War, he worked at Arawana Mills and amassed possibly the largest private collection of Colonial and Revolutionary War memorabilia in Connecticut. He died in 1901 at age 66.

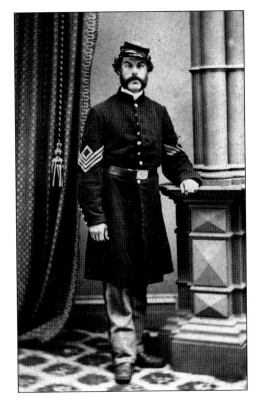

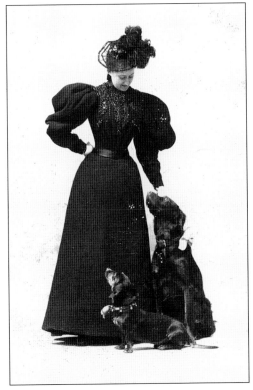

This c. 1893 photograph shows Grace Dabney Douglas with Gyp, the large dog, and Bogie. Douglas was later married to Louis DeKoven Hubbard on June 4, 1894, at the Church of the Holy Trinity in Middletown. As members of prominent families, their wedding was one of the major social events of the year, attracting society guests from New York, Providence, and Chicago.

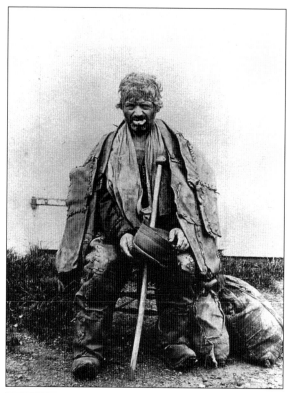

A wandering hermit who dressed entirely in leather, known to many as the Leatherman, slept in caves and lived off food donated by friends along his route. Every 34 days for about 30 years, he walked a 365-mile-long circular route between the Connecticut and Hudson Rivers. When in Middletown, he would often stop at James Fisher's house at Staddle Hill. This photograph was taken in October 1888 at the Fisher residence just west of the corner of West Street and Washington Street. The Leatherman was found dead in one of his caves in 1889.

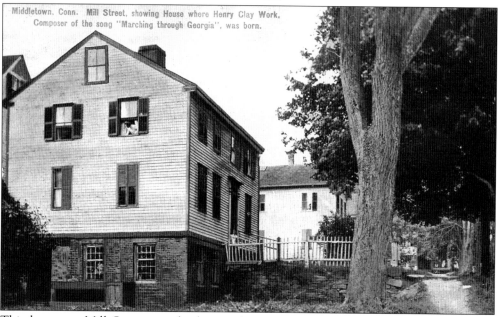

This house on Mill Street was the home of songwriter Henry Clay Work (1832–1884). A committed abolitionist, he wrote popular, patriotic songs during the Civil War, including his most famous piece, "Marching through Georgia." One song of his later years, "My Grandfather's Clock," sold almost a million copies. A bronze bust of Work sits on Main Street's South Green near the Civil War monument.

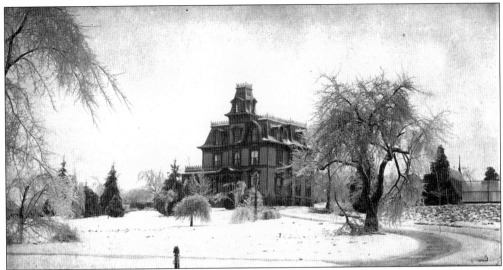

James H. Bunce, one of the most prominent businessmen in the history of Middletown, built this mansion at 107 High Street. The large brick home had a garden, orchards, linden trees, and a well that Bunce shared with his neighbors. In 1865, Bunce founded the James H. Bunce department store in Middletown and personally ran it for 42 years.

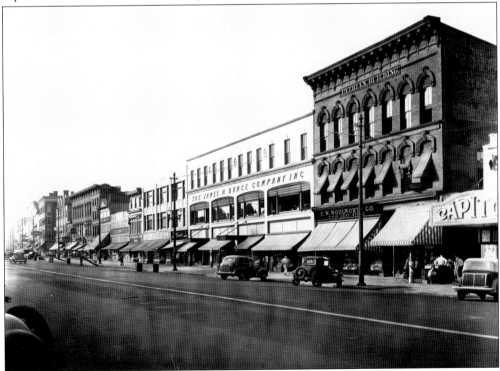

After the death of founder Bunce, this department store was retained under family control. By 1915, the store had 34 departments and 56,000 feet of floor space. This 1940 photograph shows the store next to relative newcomers, the chain stores, F. W. Woolworth on the right and W. T. Grant, four stores to the left. In the 1970s, Shapiro's, another favorite store of shoppers from Middletown and the surrounding towns, moved into the Bunce building.

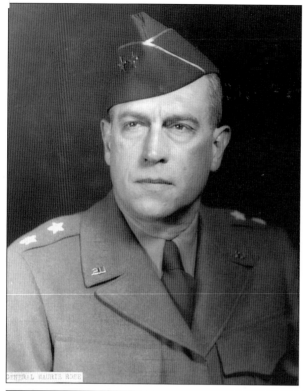

This portrait of Maj. Gen. Maurice Rose was taken on January 23, 1945, when he was commanding general of the U.S. Army's 3rd Armored Division. The son and grandson of rabbis, General Rose was born on 424 Main Street (since renumbered to 508). He was wounded in World War I and advanced in the army to become a tough tank commander in the mold of George Patton. General Rose was shot and killed by a German tank commander just weeks before the end of the war in Europe.

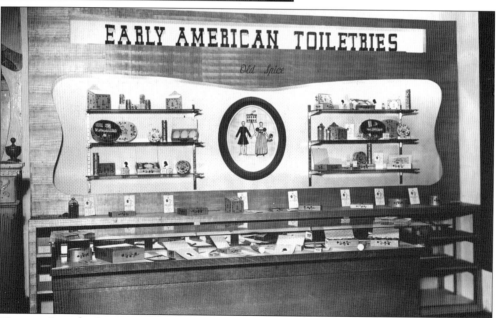

This is a photograph of a display in the Wrubel's department store on Main Street. Allie Wrubel, one of the sons of store founders Isaac and Regina Wrubel, went on to become a top Hollywood songwriter of the 1930s and 1940s. Born in Middletown in 1905, he received his diploma from Middletown High School and graduated from Wesleyan University. He won the Academy Award for the best song of 1947, "Zip-a-Dee-Doo-Dah," from the Walt Disney movie *Song of the South*.

Six

BUSINESS AND INDUSTRY

A pioneer in the use of interchangeable parts in manufacturing, Simeon North started his Middletown arms factory in about 1810 in the Staddle Hill area of the town. At the time of the War of 1812, he entered into a contract with the U.S. government to produce 20,000 pistols within five years. In 1813, he moved to Middletown and lived in a house on High Street for the rest of his life. This is a c. 1835 photograph of North.

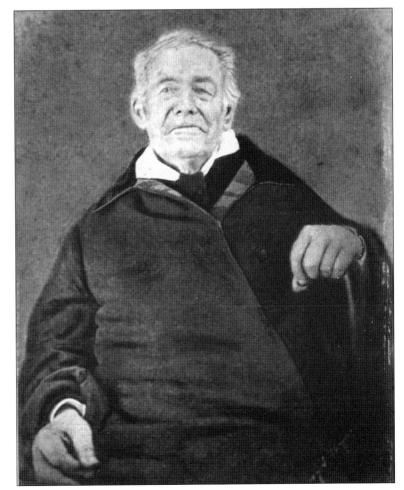

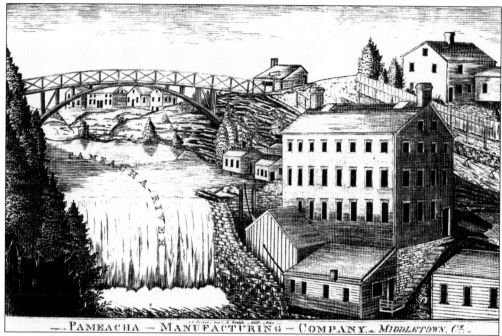

PAMEACHA — MANUFACTURING — COMPANY, MIDDLETOWN, CT.

This painting of Pameacha Manufacturing Company gives evidence of how important the Pameacha River was in powering factory machinery during the 1800s. Another factory on this river was J. R. Watkinson's woolen mill, which operated around 1814. Located on South Main Street, factories employed hundreds of workers and were largely responsible for Middletown's prosperity during the 1800s. Today the surviving brick and brownstone factories are quiet by Pameacha Pond but serve as monuments to the past.

No. 25   Baldwin Tool Company.   8 Shares.

E. W. & Starr _____ of Middletown, Conn. is entitled to Eight _____ Shares of the **Capital Stock** of the **Baldwin Tool Company**, transferable on the Books of the Company, by him, or his Attorney, on the surrender of this Certificate.

Middletown, Conn., February 1st 1854.

A. H. Jackson, Secretary.   Austin Baldwin, President.

CERTIFICATE OF STOCK.

Middletown's industrial production increased 144 percent within the decade of 1850–1860, while its workers increased from 566 to almost 1,200 people. This 1854 Baldwin Tool Company Share Certificate is a reminder of the economic boom. Other businessmen developed factories like the Sanseer Manufacturing Company that was one of Middletown's first to produce textiles and the W. H. Chapman Company that supplied hardware and sleigh bells. Immigrants arriving from Europe supplied cheap labor.

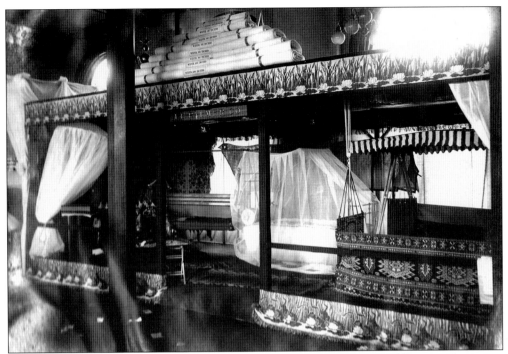

The I. E. Palmer Company had a business in New York as well as Middletown. Customers purchased many hammocks and couches in a variety of colors. Additional products were sold like hammock supports, trapeze bars, awnings, and canopy supports. The company also manufactured mosquito netting, bed canopies, screens, cloth, and crinoline dress linings.

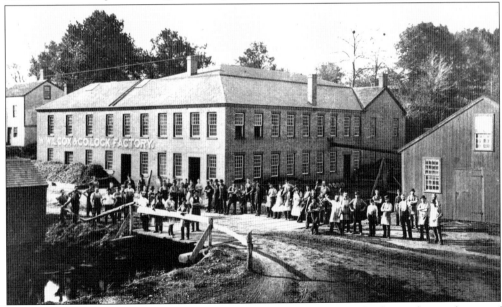

Killingworth native William Wilcox moved to Middletown at age 18, obtained several years of experience at Smith and Cooley gun makers, and in 1842, founded a lock company. This picture shows 58 of the workers at the Wilcox and Company lock factory in 1879. The business closed its doors 26 years later, a year after Wilcox's death in 1904 at age 85.

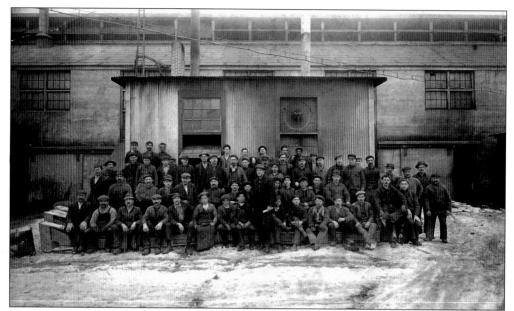

In 1847, Wilcox, Crittenden and Company, manufacturers of supplies for boat builders, specialized in iron castings and tinning work. This employee photograph is outside its factory in the South Farms district on South Main Street. Ships used its patented metal sailing grommets (for raising and lowering sails), thimbles, and hooks. The factory is now renovated housing units. Although Wilcox, Crittenden and Company is still in business today, it no longer operates in Middletown, Connecticut. Ironically it is now based in Middletown, Rhode Island.

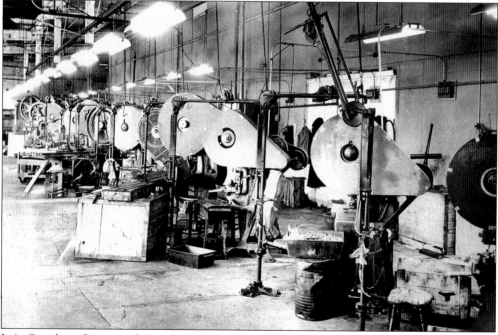

J. A. Otterbein Company, located on 55–61 Hubbard Street, was noted as a manufacturer of gun parts. This was one of many small factories that developed in the 19th and early 20th centuries and employed numerous people from Middletown and its surrounding communities.

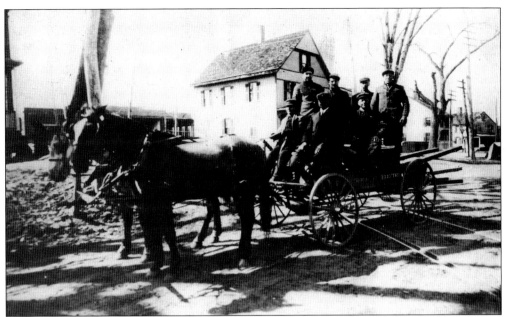

Middletown Electric Light Company employees pose in this photograph around 1908. During this time, Middletown's bill for street lighting was about $10,000 per year. At first, Main Street's lights were activated only on non-moonlit evenings. Later the city negotiated a contract with the Electric Light Company to have all lights on each evening and for the city to receive a 30¢ rebate per evening for each light that malfunctioned.

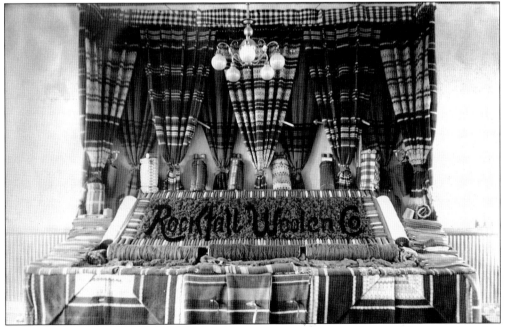

Incorporated in 1882, Rockfall Woolen Company specialized in the manufacture of woolen blankets. It performed all steps of the process at its plant, receiving raw wool, dying, spinning, weaving, and finishing. The waters of Little River supplied 50 horsepower, while a 40-horsepower steam engine filled the rest of its energy needs.

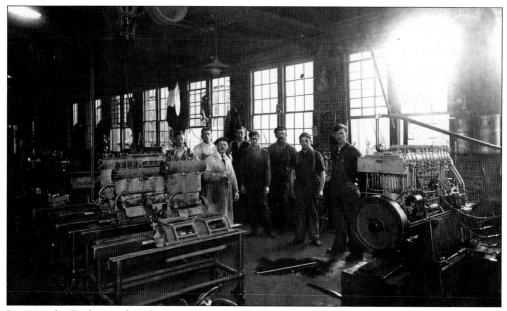

In 1914, the Frisbee and Heft Motor Company located on College Street employed John Arthur Otterbein, back row, third from the left, and foreman Bud Hubbard, in the white shop coat. The 1908 business directory advertised a four-cycle 3-80-horsepower motor that was fully guaranteed and a 1928 directory advertisement featured Frisbee and Heft motors.

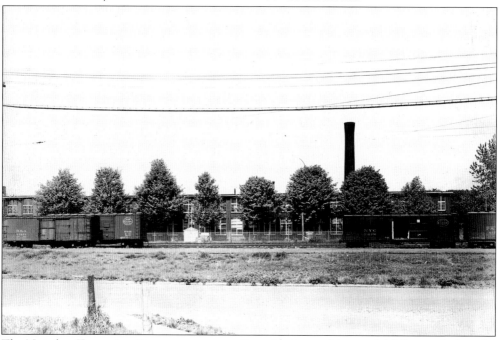

The Noiseless Typewriter Company was manufacturing its machines in Middletown before the 1920s. Many models were patented and advertised as quiet, noise-free machines. They had the word "Middletown" imprinted on their bodies. In 1924, Remington Rand acquired this company and continued the production of typewriters at this plant until 1936. This photograph was taken in about 1928. Today the plant is the home of several small companies.

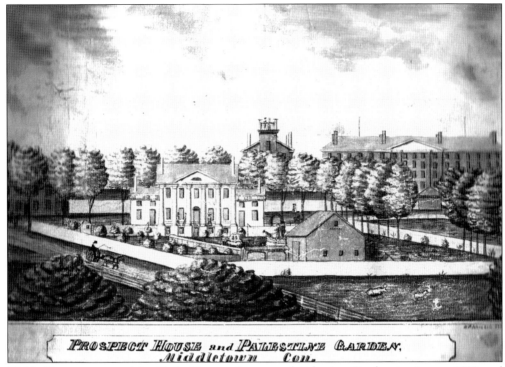

PROSPECT HOUSE and PALESTINE GARDEN, Middletown Con.

Webb Place was owned by Heth Camp, who opened Palestine Garden in August 1828 and continued until Webb's Preparatory School for Boys moved in 1833. A price of 12.5¢ bought admittance to these public gardens, a stroll viewing plants brought from the Holy Land, and music. Viewed here in 1831 are Prospect House, Palestine Gardens, and Wesleyan's College Row in the background.

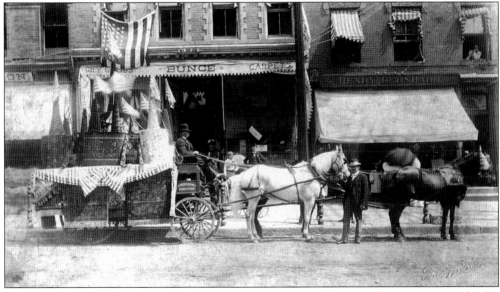

Celebrating Barbecue Day in 1896, James H. Bunce's team of horses pulls a creative rug display on Main Street in front of Bunce's dry goods store. Starting his store in 1865, Bunce personally ran it until shortly before his death, 43 years later.

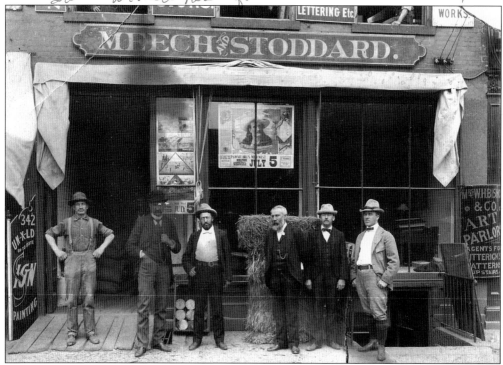

Louis worked here for a while in 1946 – 1947 Part time

Six men stand outside Meech and Stoddard, a grain and feed store, around 1900. A large sign in the front window advertises two performances of Pawnee Bill's Wild West Show to be held in Middletown. A business above advertises painting signs and wagon lettering. To the right are Mrs. W. H. Bishop and Company and agents for Butterick's Patterns.

G. T. Meech and O. E. Stoddard established their store in 1870. It was located at 340 Main Street and sold flour, grain, feed, and field seed. A $28 receipt from June 1, 1889, is for 10 sacks each of bran, meal, and gluten. It stipulated that all transactions were for cash and that all claims must be made within five days after receipt of goods.

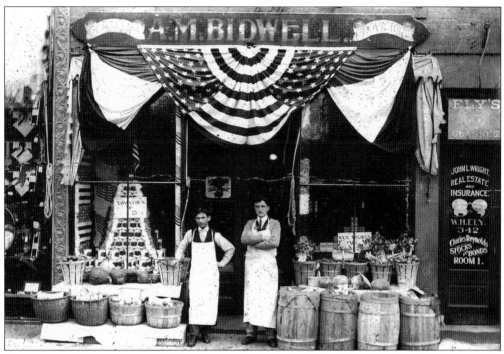

Groceries and provisions could be purchased at A. M. Bidwell's store. To the right in this photograph are John Wright's Real Estate and Insurance and Charles Reynold's stock and bond business. Squash and other fresh produce are in baskets outside the store, while windows display items like canned tomatoes, prunes, and Tetley Teas.

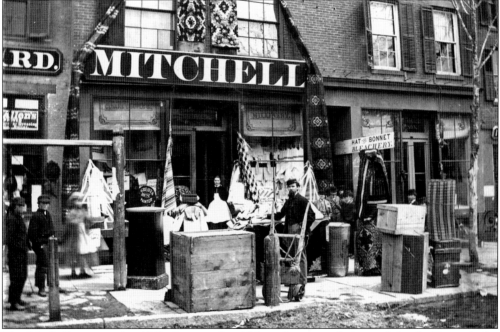

The Mitchell store in this 1860 photograph sold hats, bonnets, cloaks, and shawls. To catch the passerby's attention is a prominent sign "beachery." This store is now Smith and Bishel Company.

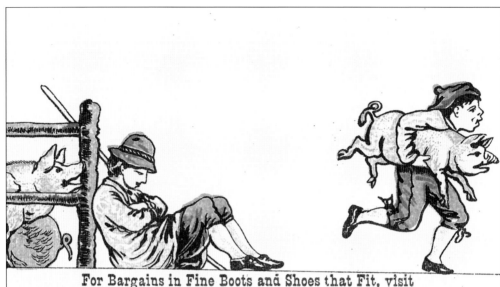

For Bargains in Fine Boots and Shoes that Fit, visit
CLARKE'S CASH STORE, No. 104 MAIN STREET
MIDDLETOWN.

Many lithographs and advertisements appeared in stores where one shopped, in newspapers, in the annual Middletown-Portland city directories, and as fliers. As today, they try to capture ones attention through humor or originality. Here is an example of a shoe business at 104 Main Street that dealt only in cash.

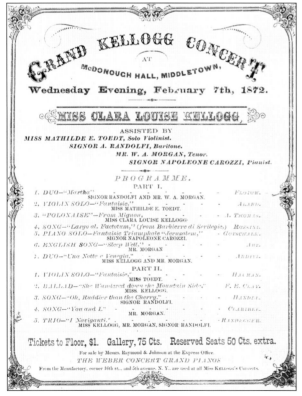

This broadside advertises an 1872 performance by world-renowned opera singer Clara Louise Kellogg at McDonough Hall on Main Street. Kellogg (1842–1916) is considered the first United States–born operatic talent. Two years after this Middletown engagement, she founded her own successful opera company and managed it until her retirement in 1887. McDonough Hall was built in the 1850s and tickets for this performance ranged between 50¢ and $1.

The McDonough Opera House hosted this Irish play on St. Patrick's Day in 1885. Backers included the Meriden Literary Association and the Knights of Columbus. The Knights of Columbus was founded in New Haven only three years previously and Middletown's "Forest City Council" was the third council formed.

McDonough Opera House,

Tuesday Ev'g, Mar. 17, '85

PRODUCTION BY THE

Meriden ❋ Literary ❋ Association

under the auspices of

Forest City Council, No. 3, K. of C.

of the Popular Irish Drama in Five Acts,

entitled,

Kathleen Mavourneen

CAST OF CHARACTERS:

KATHLEEN O'CONNOR,	Miss LIZZIE McFARLAND
KITTY O'LAVERY,	Miss MAY SCULLY
MISS DOROTHY KAVANAGH,	Miss EMMA RYAN
MEG MARSLOGH,	Mrs. NEWMAN
BERNARD KAVANAGH,	Mr. J. D. BERGEN
DAVID O'CONNOR,	Mr. JAMES QUINLAN
FATHER O'CASSIDY,	Mr. JOHN F. SEERY
TERENCE O'MOORE,	Mr. T. L. REILLY
BILL BUTTON CAP,	Mr. J. M. FLETCHER
CAPTAIN CLEARFIELD,	Mr. CHARLES E. BIBEAU
BLACK RODY,	Mr. JAMES J. FLYNN
RED BARNEY,	Mr. H. H. DALY
MR. McCUBBAN,	Mr. G. CLARK
DENNIS,	Mr. E. F. KORN

Soldiers, Peasants, &c.

SYNOPSIS:

ACT I.—St. Patrick's Eve. The Happy Home of Farmer O'Conner. The Landlords Visit.

ACT II.—Kathleen's Dream. The timely arrival of Father O'Cassidy.

ACT III.—The Attempted Murder. Arrest of Terrence.

ACT IV.—Kathleen's Remorse.

ACT V.—St. Patricks Day. Happy Finale.

Doors Open at 7.   Curtain Rises at 8.

PRICES, 25, 35 & 50 Cts.

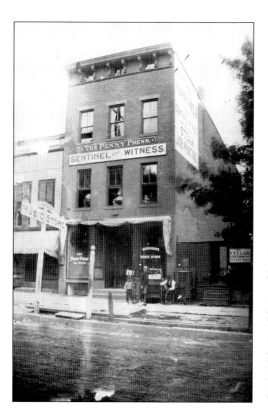

Middletown was the eighth town in Connecticut to have a printing press. The *Middlesex Gazette* began publishing in 1785. This photograph is of an unpaved Main Street with horse hitching posts in front of the *Penny Press*, a daily paper eventually becoming the daily *Middletown Press,* and the *Sentinel and Witness,* a weekly paper published every Saturday. On the ground floor is Kennison's Music Store while C. C. Clark, locksmith, gunsmith, and pattern maker, is in the building to the right.

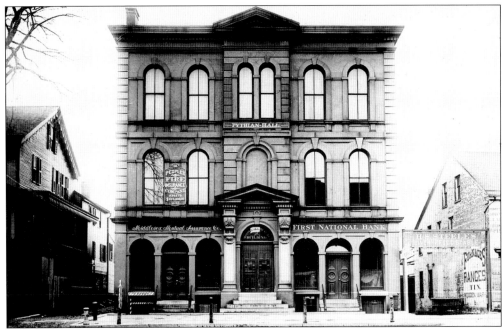

Pythian Hall provided space for the Middlesex Mutual Assurance Company on the left ground floor and the First National Bank on the right. The next buildings to the right are H. S. Steele's Livery and Feed Stable and a store that sold furnaces, kitchen furnishings, and bird cages.

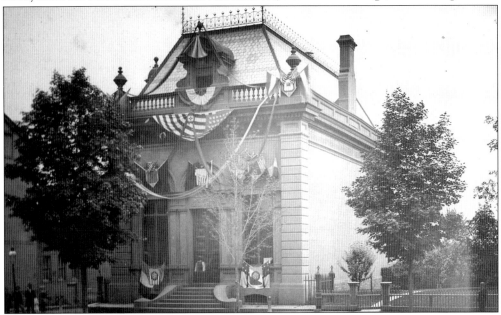

Middletown Bank was chartered by the Connecticut General Assembly in 1795 and opened in 1801 with Elijah Hubbard as its first president and Timothy Southmayd as a cashier. The Middletown Savings Bank, incorporated in May 1825, was the third mutual savings bank in Connecticut. From 1825 to 1832, Nehemiah Hubbard was the first president and E. G. Southmayd its secretary-treasurer. It is photographed here wearing a proud 1884 centennial banner for the City of Middletown's incorporation anniversary. Eventually Middletown Savings became Liberty Bank.

This photograph shows Middletown National Bank in 1884. The Middletown Bank became the Middletown National Bank and was the 11th oldest Connecticut bank and the 6th oldest national bank in the country. One story states that Hartford banks were not pleased that it opened, so they bought bank bills in circulation. Hubbard, its president, heard about this, so he had on hand a large amount of copper cents. However the redeemed notes caused heavy coinage, over-loading the vehicle and causing a break down as it returned to Hartford.

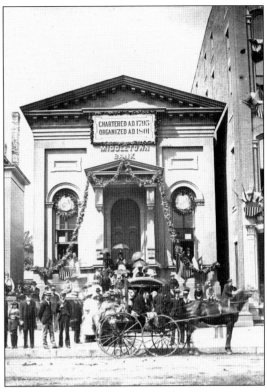

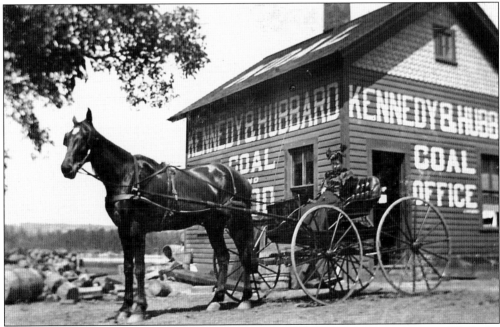

Posed in front of Kennedy and Hubbard is a finely dressed woman in an open carriage. While the company's office was at 114 Center Street, its yard was at the foot of Union Street. Kennedy and Hubbard dealt in coal and wood. It would do both flagging and curb stone as well as transport deliveries in its wagons.

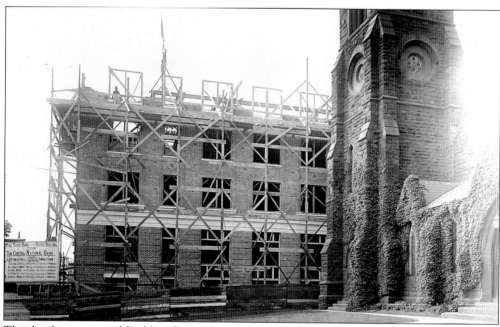

This brick commercial building built in 1915 on Main Street housed Central National Bank (1865–1955) and was adjacent to the Church of the Holy Trinity. It eventually became Hartford National Bank and Trust, which conducted business in the same location for many years. Currently Webster Bank resides here. On the right side of Holy Trinity was City Savings Bank. The building today houses the Middlesex County Chamber of Commerce.

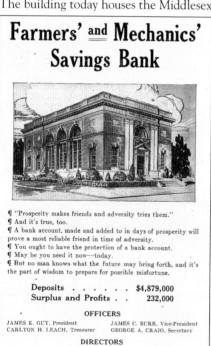

Farmers' and Mechanics' Savings Bank

¶ "Prosperity makes friends and adversity tries them."
¶ And it's true, too.
¶ A bank account, made and added to in days of prosperity will prove a most reliable friend in time of adversity.
¶ You ought to have the protection of a bank account.
¶ May be you need it now—today.
¶ But no man knows what the future may bring forth, and it's the part of wisdom to prepare for possible misfortune.

Deposits $4,879,000
Surplus and Profits . . 232,000

OFFICERS

JAMES K. GUY, President   JAMES C. BURR, Vice-President
CARLTON H. LEACH, Treasurer   GEORGE A. CRAIG, Secretary

DIRECTORS

George T. Meech	William W. Wilcox	Joseph Merriam
James K. Guy	Francis A. Beach	Willis E. Terrill
Edward S. Coe	James C. Burr	Thos. W. McDowell

195 Main Street   Middletown, Conn.

Farmers' and Mechanics' Savings Bank, with Middletown as its main headquarters, was the second largest depository in Middletown. Founded in 1858, it was a Connecticut-chartered, FDIC-insured savings bank with 12 banking offices serving four Connecticut counties. It was acquired by Citizen's Bank in 1996. In this 1915 advertisement, it had almost $5 million in deposits and a surplus of $232,000 with its location at 195 Main Street. Citizens Bank is on the site today.

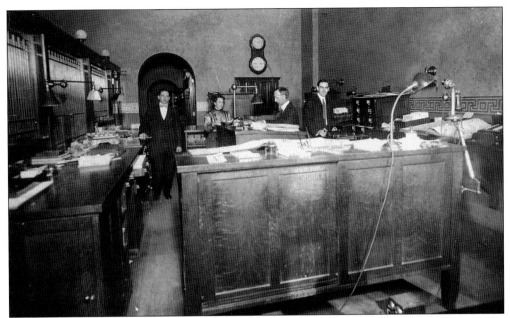

This is a photograph of Middletown City National Bank around 1910. On the left are the teller windows while the back arch is the unlocked vault. All four workers are dressed in conservative business attire, and much of their work required a well-lit workspace and accurate, neat penmanship for accounts and ledgers. An old-fashioned telephone can be seen on the right of this photograph.

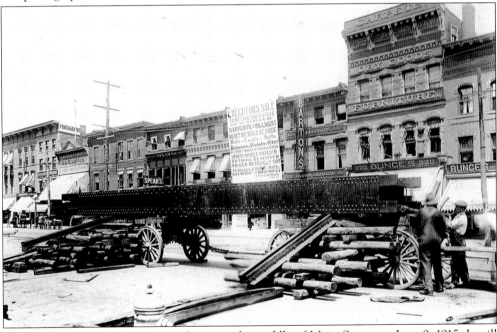

A flatbed car is unloading a main beam in the middle of Main Street on June 9, 1915. It will be used in the construction of the new Central National Bank building. Considered the first modern office building in Middletown, the bank's marble cornerstone was laid by Mayor Revilo Markham two weeks later.

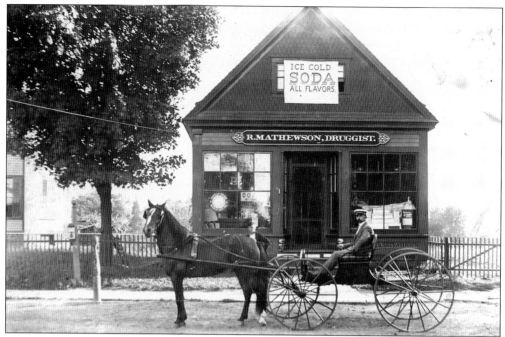

Stopping in the South Farms area of town to show off his horse and buggy, a gentleman poses at the corner of East Main Street and Silver Street in front of Mathewson's Drug Store. Registered pharmacist Randolph Mathewson, a Durham native, first opened this pharmacy in September 1893. In addition to medicine, the store sold toilet articles, soda, and 5¢ Fontella Cigars.

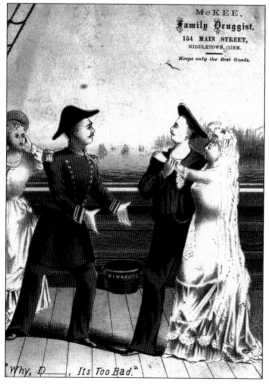

Main Street's McKee Drug Store uses a picture from Gilbert and Sullivan's 1878 comic opera *H.M.S. Pinafore* to attract attention in this trade card.

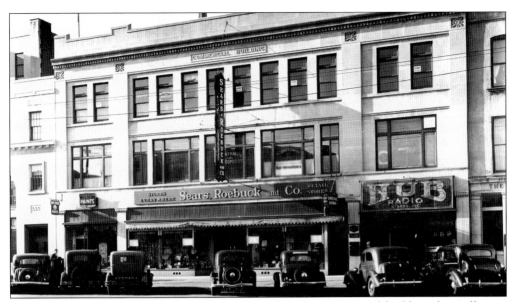

In 1937, Sears, Roebuck and Company was housed in the commercial building that still is on Main Street. This retail store advertised itself as having stores everywhere. On the left is Bay State Paint with the Hartford Courant above on the second floor, while on the right is Hub Radio Store with Binec Beauty Salon above.

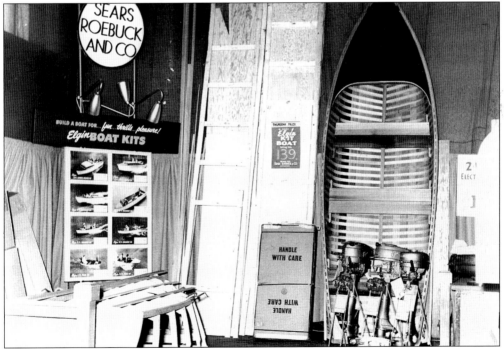

Sears, Roebuck and Company was paired with Elgin products for years. Sears offered this 1954 display, to entice its customers into buying one of its Elgin kit boat models and Elgin boat motors. It promoted a 14-foot kit, which cost $139 to build. With the Connecticut River nearby, its advertisement to build an Elgin boat for "fun, thrills, and pleasure" grabbed customers' attention. These products are still being used today.

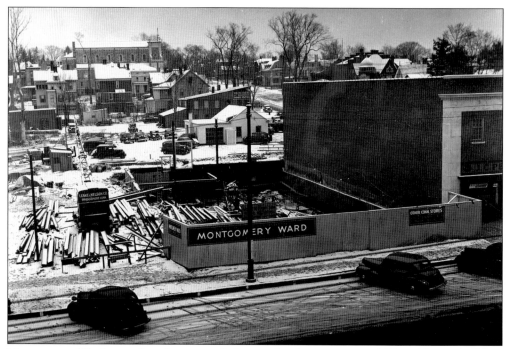

Montgomery Ward started as the country's first mail-order business in 1872 and began building a chain of retail stores in the 1920s. Building downtown stores, such as this store on Main Street in 1938, it became one of the top department store chains by the 1950s. After 1960, as competitors constructed many new stores in suburban malls, Montgomery Ward stayed with downtown stores, lost market share, and eventually went out of business.

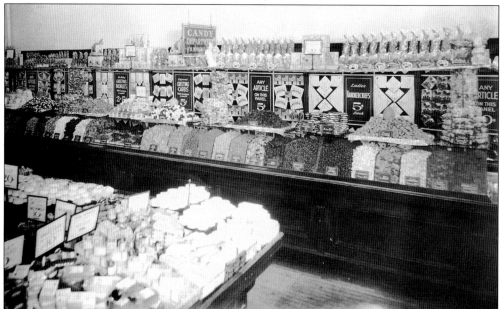

Here in F. W. Woolworth's Main Street store around 1938, the candy department is filled with chocolate bunnies and bins of mouthwatering cookies. Posted on the board behind the sweets are 5¢ ladies handkerchiefs and 2½¢ birthday greeting booklets.

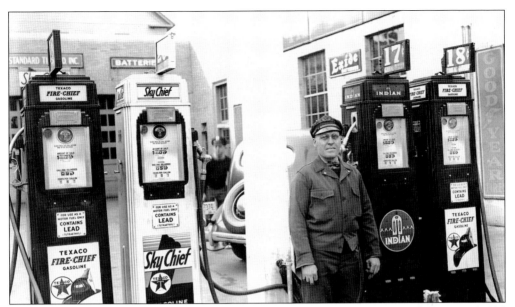

One of the major oil companies at the time, Texaco's Middletown station is seen here around 1938 selling three grades of gasoline for less than 20¢ per gallon: Fire-Chief, Indian, and its newest, Sky Chief. One advertisement for Sky Chief featured an airplane pilot and the words, "On the ground he'll want this new gasoline." After filling up their cars on Sunday, people would head home to listen to comedian Eddie Cantor's radio program, which was sponsored by Texaco.

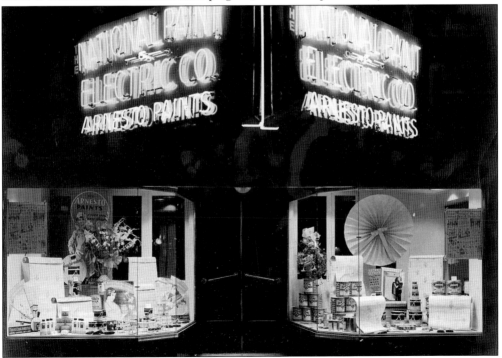

The National Paint store, shown here in a c. 1939 photograph, gave most of its window display over to the Arnesto Paints product line. With the paint slogan, "Cover more, last longer," Arnesto also supplied porch and deck enamel as well as floor wax.

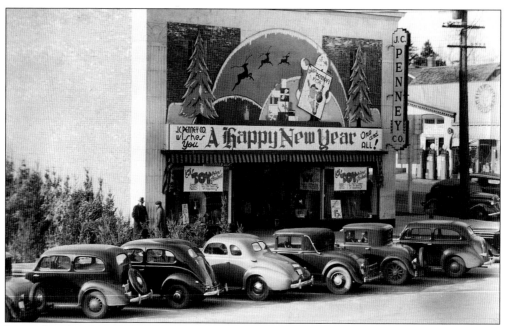

Located at the corner of Main Street and Washington Street, the J. C. Penney Company was a thriving retail business serving Middletown and the surrounding community. In this 1940 photograph, a plethora of cars are parked outside this store as customers are enticed inside to take advantage of the holiday sales.

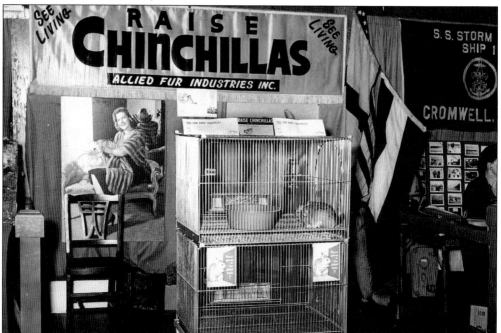

Chinchillas are small South American rodents hunted and raised for their soft fur, which is primarily used in the manufacture of coats. Hunting led to the near extinction of the animal in the wild in the 1940s. This is a 1950s photograph of a display that tried to encourage local residents to make money raising Chinchillas.

Seven

FOOD AND LODGING

One can get a sense of a bustling Main Street with its stagecoach and horse-drawn buggy, along with its three story buildings and abundant chimneys, providing heat and welcoming accommodations for guests in the late 1880s. On this 1885 statement, charges indicate that a family's night stay was $2.25 for room and board. Earlier in the century, Middletown had three hotels: the Mansion House, the Central Hotel, and the Farmers and Mechanics Hotel.

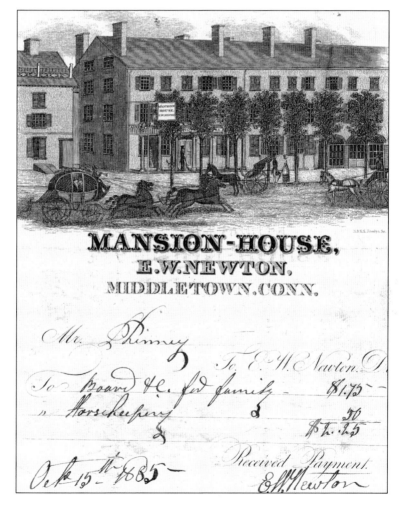

MANSION-HOUSE,
E.W. NEWTON,
MIDDLETOWN, CONN.

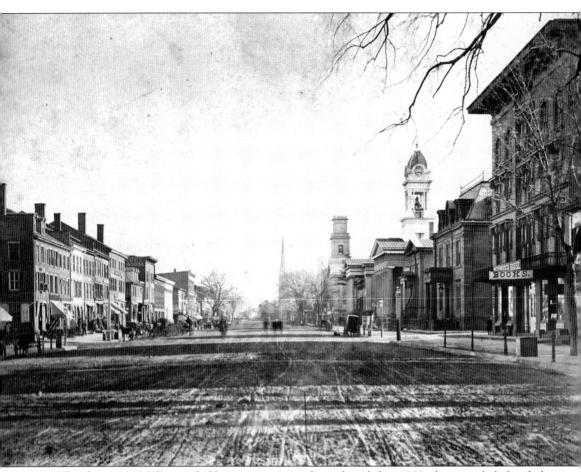

The four-story McDonough House appears at the right of this 1888 photograph behind the "books" sign. Opened in 1857, it had louvered window shutters and an iron balcony encircling the second floor. In the late 1880s, its hotel rooms could accommodate about 150 guests and its banquet facilities were the best Middletown could offer to local and statewide organizations. It was replaced by the Liberty Bank Building in 1928. The large white building to the left was the courthouse.

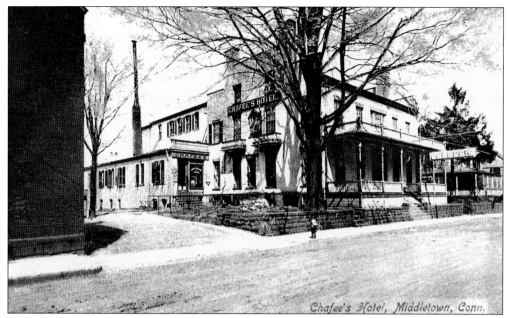

Chafee's Hotel, Middletown, Conn.

A residence, with a central hall downstairs and marble-mantled fireplaces, constructed for Henry Carrington around 1812 at 74 Court Street was the first time a building was placed here since 1764. This 1909 postcard of Chafee's Hotel had a 1¢ postage stamp and was written to show where a friend worked. Charles Chafee owned the hotel from 1903 until 1935, when he sold it to the Sons of Italy Mutual Aid Society.

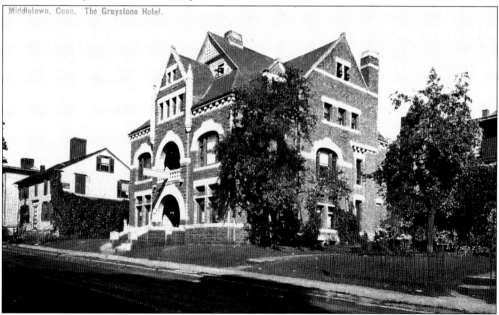

Middletown, Conn. The Graystone Hotel.

The attractive appearance of Graystone Hotel at 150 College Street provided a stop in September 1910 for a family who motored down from Hartford in their automobile. They could have chosen other hotels at this time, such as the Chafee Hotel at 74 Court Street or the four hotels on Main Street, Main Park Hotel at 124, American Hotel at 301, Hotel Middletown at 524, or Hotel Mattabesett at 529.

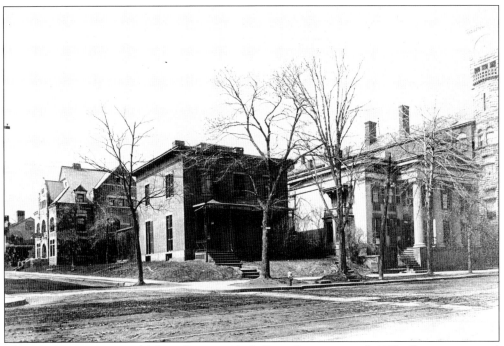

The northwest corner of Main Street and College Street around 1910 illustrates several multistoried buildings, from left to right, Graystone Hotel on College Street and on Main Street, the former home of Dr. William Bell, the Nehemiah Hubbard Jr. house, and the municipal building with its clock tower.

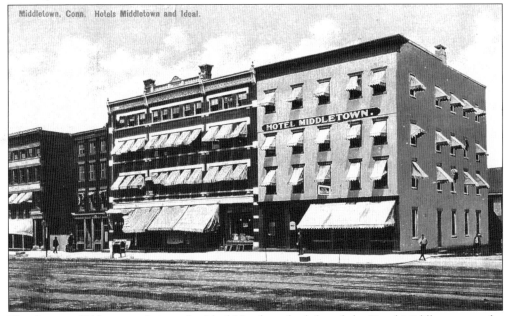

This January 1913 postcard views the Ideal Hotel on the left and the Hotel Middletown on the right. Located at 524 Main Street, Hotel Middletown's proprietor at the time was M. Luther Anderson. The Hotel Middletown was a four-story brick building with striped awnings as were most buildings during this time.

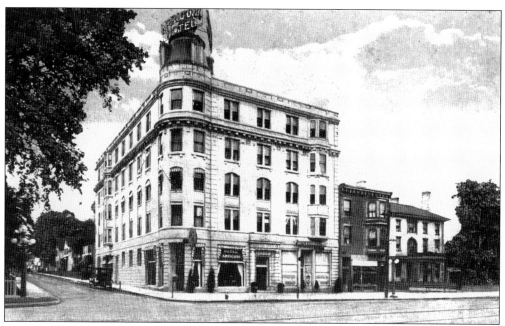

Arrigoni Hotel at the corner of Main Street and Liberty Street looks much the same today as it did 80 years earlier. In this 1921 postcard, the prominent sign atop the building attracts guests. Located nearby in Middletown's north end are St. John's Church, Riverside Cemetery, Mortimer Cemetery, and Middletown Fire Station No. 1, now known as Middletown Fire Station Headquarters.

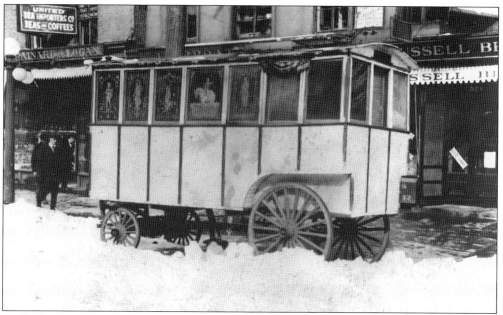

In the late 1800s and early 1900s, Spencer C. Page's food cart was a popular sight on Main Street. After arriving at the spot pictured here in 1917, "Pop" Page would unhitch his old, reliable horse, who would head back home by himself. Pop would then hook up the electric line to his cart and be in business cooking and selling sandwiches to townsfolk and visitors. At 15 years old, Jack Fitzgerald began working for Pop and opened his own restaurant in 1922.

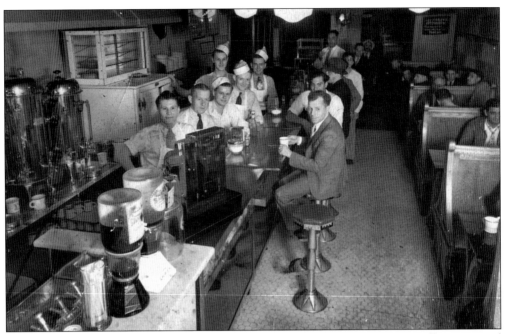

For 44 years, Jack Fitzgerald operated Jack's Lunch on 434 Main Street, selling steamed cheeseburgers cooked in a tall copper box filled with simmering water for 18 tin trays of square ground-beef patties. Cheddar cheeseburgers cost an additional 5¢. The 1933 night crew pictured here includes, from left to right, Butch Rolish, Bill Bruggen, Harry Schultz, Jack Dunn, John O'Rourke, and Eddie Skinski (behind).

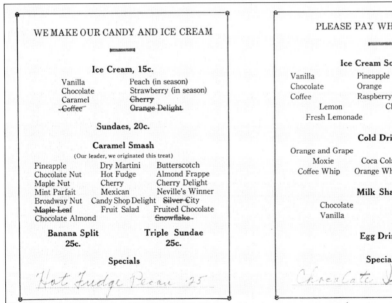

WE MAKE OUR CANDY AND ICE CREAM

Ice Cream, 15c.

Vanilla	Peach (in season)
Chocolate	Strawberry (in season)
Caramel	~~Cherry~~
~~Coffee~~	~~Orange Delight~~

Sundaes, 20c.

Caramel Smash
(Our leader, we originated this treat)

Pineapple	Dry Martini	Butterscotch
Chocolate Nut	Hot Fudge	Almond Frappe
Maple Nut	Cherry	Cherry Delight
Mint Parfait	Mexican	Neville's Winner
Broadway Nut	Candy Shop Delight	~~Silver City~~
~~Maple Leaf~~	Fruit Salad	Fruited Chocolate
Chocolate Almond		~~Snowflake~~

Banana Split	Triple Sundae
25c.	25c.

Specials

Hot Fudge Pecan '25

PLEASE PAY WHEN SERVED

Ice Cream Soda, 15c

Vanilla	Pineapple	Strawberry
Chocolate	Orange	Sarsaparilla
Coffee	Raspberry	Cherry
Lemon	Chocolate Mint	
Fresh Lemonade	Fresh Orangeade	

Cold Drinks

Orange and Grape		Lemon and Lime
Moxie	Coca Cola	Grape Juice
Coffee Whip	Orange Whip	Ginger Ale

Milk Shakes

Chocolate	Coffee
Vanilla	Malted Milk

Egg Drinks

Specials

Chocolate Imperial 20

Neville's Candy Shop, located on 370 Main Street, was a popular and crowded meeting place during the 1920s and 1930s. Many local teenagers, as well as those who traveled by bus from surrounding towns, met up at "Nifty" and devoured the delicious homemade treats that the establishment offered.

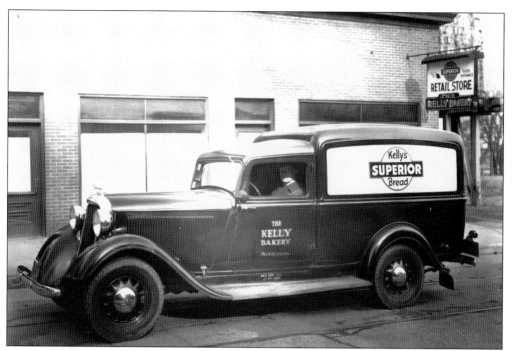

The Kelly Bakery, on 46–48 Rapallo Avenue, was the proud owner of a new delivery truck in this 1938 photograph. Other bakeries popular for their bread, hard rolls, or donuts were Shaffer Bakery and Field's Bakery on Main Street, Marino's Bakery on Ferry Street, Lastrina's and Middlesex Baking Company on Union Street, and Modern Bakery on Sumner Street.

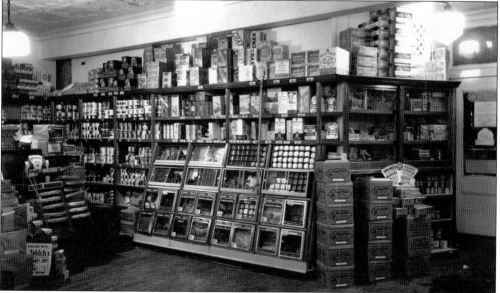

In this 1938 photograph, Economy Meat, located on 189 East Main Street, sold a variety of other products to its customers like Milk-Bone dog biscuits, Smith Brothers' cough drops, Royal Lunch milk crackers (that have since been discontinued), and Uneeda Bakers cookies. The sign by its No Bake Kraft dinners offers a free Walt Disney *Snow White and the Seven Dwarfs* glass with a Kraft dinner purchase.

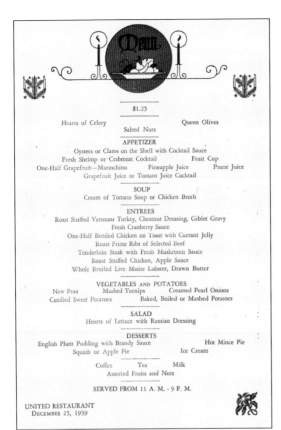

Menu

$1.25

Hearts of Celery   Queen Olives
Salted Nuts

APPETIZER
Oysters or Clams on the Shell with Cocktail Sauce
Fresh Shrimp or Crabmeat Cocktail   Fruit Cup
One-Half Grapefruit—Maraschino   Pineapple Juice   Prune Juice
Grapefruit Juice or Tomato Juice Cocktail

SOUP
Cream of Tomato Soup or Chicken Broth

ENTREES
Roast Stuffed Vermont Turkey, Chestnut Dressing, Giblet Gravy
Fresh Cranberry Sauce
One-Half Broiled Chicken on Toast with Currant Jelly
Roast Prime Ribs of Selected Beef
Tenderloin Steak with Fresh Mushroom Sauce
Roast Stuffed Chicken, Apple Sauce
Whole Broiled Live Maine Lobster, Drawn Butter

VEGETABLES AND POTATOES
New Peas   Mashed Turnips   Creamed Pearl Onions
Candied Sweet Potatoes   Baked, Boiled or Mashed Potatoes

SALAD
Hearts of Lettuce with Russian Dressing

DESSERTS
English Plum Pudding with Brandy Sauce   Hot Mince Pie
Squash or Apple Pie   Ice Cream

Coffee   Tea   Milk
Assorted Fruits and Nuts

SERVED FROM 11 A. M. - 9 P. M.

UNITED RESTAURANT
DECEMBER 25, 1939

After eating at the United, patrons in 1938 could attend one of the two theaters in town that had a total seating capacity of 2,669. An additional vacant theater had 1,000 more seats. At this time, Middletown had about 25,000 people and its retail establishments served twice that number in a radius of about 45 miles.

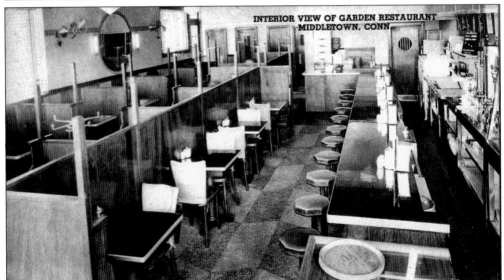

This postcard of the interior of the Garden Restaurant, located in a busy intersection of Middletown on the northwest corner of Main and Washington Streets, advertised itself as famous for its seafood dishes. It popularity was due to its location and reasonable prices. It became another landmark in Middletown, staying in business for years serving the after-movie crowd soups, eggs and omelets, hot and cold sandwiches, and many specialty drinks.

Eight

TRANSPORTATION

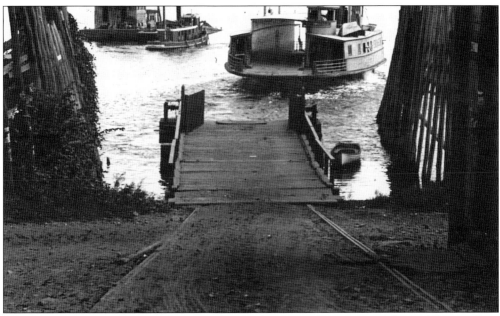

The ferry made it easy for travelers to get across the river. This picture of the Middletown ferry slip dates between 1880 and 1890. Many passengers relied on this mode of transportation before the 1896 road bridge was constructed.

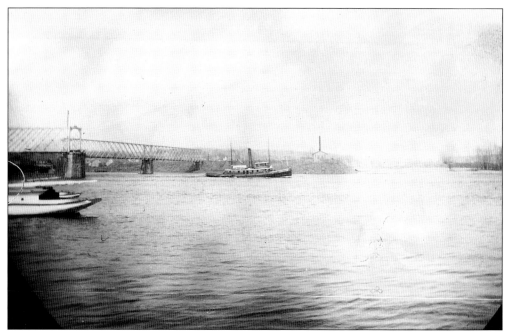

The *Trio* is viewed passing through the calm Connecticut River waters in 1893. The Air Line Bridge in the background handled trains traveling between New Haven and Willimantic. The bridge was built in 1872 by Pittsburgh's Keystone Bridge Company for $400,000.

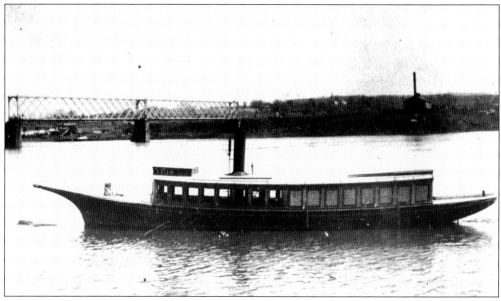

Ferrying passengers, animals, and merchandise across the Connecticut River from Middletown to nearby communities was important. Raymond Baldwin, a Connecticut governor, U.S. senator, and chief justice of the state supreme court, recalled memories from his youth in Middletown, "the *Ward*, an early-vintage wooden tugboat, then later the *Mabel* and the *Sachem* with its tall stacks and two-masts, soon replaced by the *Spartan*, the *Comet*, and the *Onrust*, which was named after the ship of Adrian Block who discovered the Connecticut River." A tugboat passes by the Air Line Bridge in this *c.* 1895 photograph.

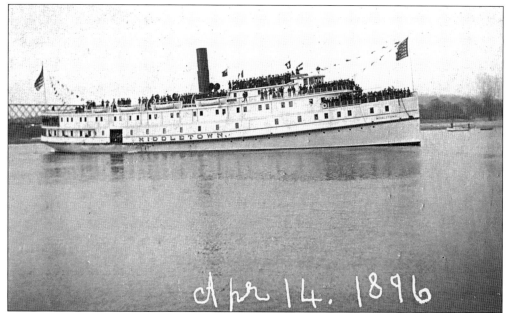

This April 14, 1896, photograph was taken of the boat *Middletown* on her first trip to New York City from Hartford. In later years, the *Middletown* would transport passengers from Hartford to Middletown in the evenings for moonlight sails on the steamboat *Falcon*. The *Middletown* was ultimately scrapped in 1938 after years of competition from trains and automobiles.

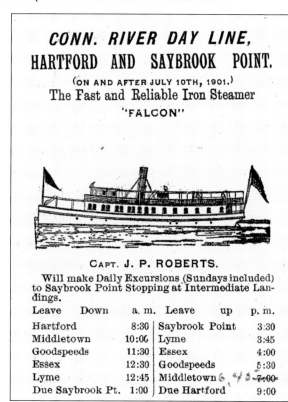

CONN. RIVER DAY LINE,
HARTFORD AND SAYBROOK POINT.
(ON AND AFTER JULY 10TH, 1901.)
The Fast and Reliable Iron Steamer
"FALCON"

CAPT. **J. P. ROBERTS.**

Will make Daily Excursions (Sundays included) to Saybrook Point Stopping at Intermediate Landings.

Leave Down	a. m.	Leave up	p. m.
Hartford	8:30	Saybrook Point	3:30
Middletown	10:00	Lyme	3:45
Goodspeeds	11:30	Essex	4:00
Essex	12:30	Goodspeeds	5:30
Lyme	12:45	Middletown	7:00
Due Saybrook Pt.	1:00	Due Hartford	9:00

This is a 1901 flyer for the river steamer *Falcon* that traveled the Connecticut River between Hartford and Saybrook Point. Round-trip fare was $1. Round-trip between Middletown and Saybrook Point was 75¢. Children were charged half fare.

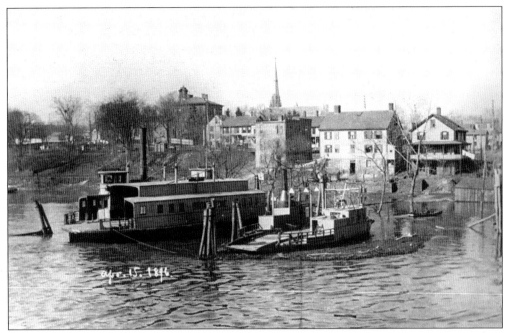

In this April 15, 1896, photograph, one can see the ferry landing, the steeple of St. John's Catholic Church, and, on the far left, the Riverside Cemetery. The residential neighborhood pictured here was mostly occupied by immigrant families from Ireland. Today four lanes of the Route 9 highway cut off the city from the river.

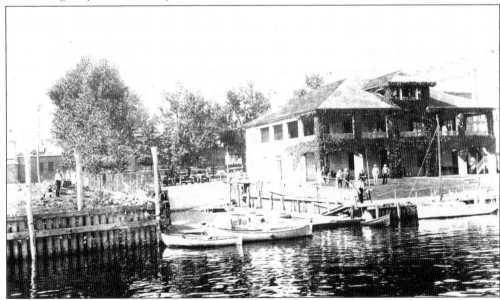

The Middletown Yacht Club is pictured here around 1924. Originally known in 1896 as the Mattabesett Canoe Club, it became the Middletown Yacht Club after it bought land and a clubhouse for around $5,700. The yacht club has since moved downriver, and the original building is a restaurant with docking facilities available. The area is still prone to the river's spring flood. Alongside is Middletown's renovated Harbor Park, which is a popular spot for strolling down the boardwalk as one enjoys the scenic view of the river.

David Lyman was the first president of
the Air Line Railroad that connected
New Haven, Middletown, and
Willimantic. In addition, he founded
the Metropolitan Washing Machine
Company in Middlefield and built
the Lyman family home. Today the
Lyman family is best known for its
famed orchards.

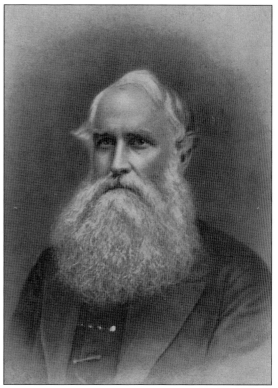

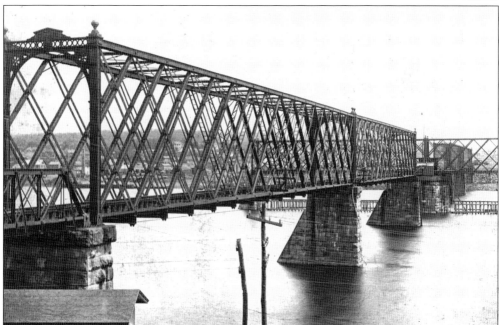

The Air Line Bridge was completed in 1872. It fulfilled the dream of local businessmen to have
the means to transport their goods by train across the Connecticut River at Middletown. This
bridge opened to allow tall vessels to pass through safely; however, it was recorded that the large
pillars were hazardous during foggy days.

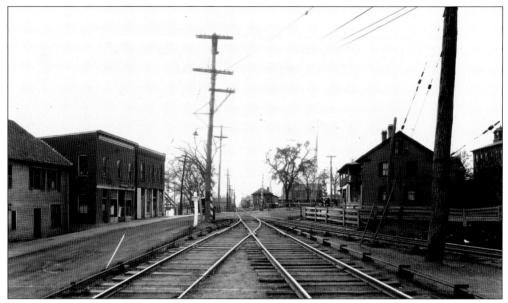

This is a view of the railroad tracks at Bridge Street. One of the earlier promoters of the railroad for the Middletown area was David Lyman (1820–1871). A member of the Middlefield Lyman orchard family, he founded the New Haven, Middletown and Willimantic Railroad, also known as the Air Line. It was designed as a railway leg for passengers traveling between New York City and Boston. Lyman's competition was the New York, New Haven, and Hartford Railroad. In order to get the support of one additional town, Lyman's influence resulted in the state legislature splitting Middlefield off from Middletown in 1866. Lyman died just before his railroad was completed, and the company was sold to his competitor.

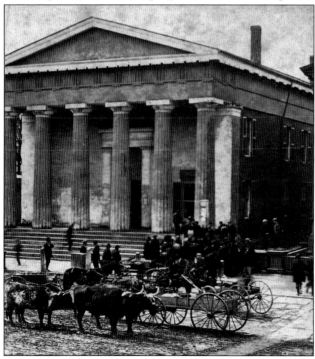

This photograph of the courthouse on Main Street includes some ancient forms of transportation. Although this is a 19th-century picture, horses were still commonly used for travel in the 1920s and 1930s, especially in the rural areas of Middletown.

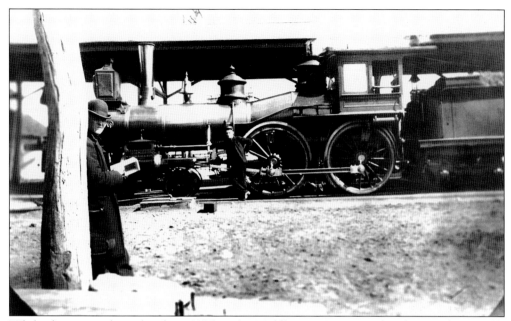

While this man takes a break in 1895 at the Middletown Union Railroad Depot by Rapallo Avenue, he could view the changes by the riverfront as multistory homes were built to accommodate new arrivals who sought work in Middletown. The railroad was an important means of transportation to Hartford, New Haven, New York, and the surrounding towns.

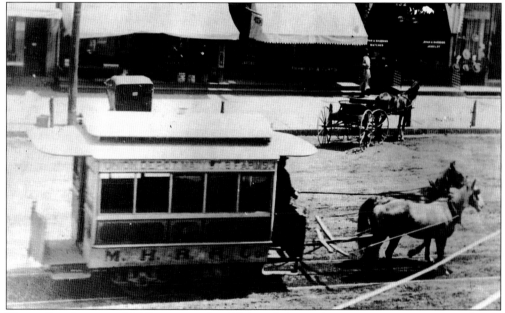

The trolleys began in Middletown in the 1880s with horse-drawn, open streetcars transferring passengers from Main Street to the railroad station. The Middletown Horse Railroad Company (MHRR) was established on September 14, 1886. Shown here is one of its trolley cars in front of Main Street's Parmelee and Curtis and a jewelry store at 132 Main Street. Instead of a Sunday automobile drive, a family could go trolley riding. The conductor would ring the bell, collect the nickel for fare, place it in his big leather pocket, and then they would be off.

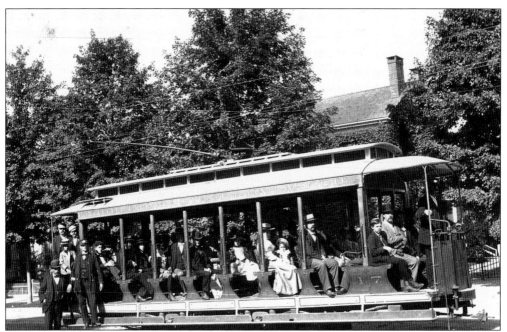

The first electric railway line started on December 22, 1894. It was given the name Middletown Street Railway in 1896. It extended 4.5 miles, with terminals at the railroad passenger station in the north end, South Main Street, South Farms, and the Asylum. Middletown Street Railway Company's No. 17 trolley car is shown here. When buses became more economical, trolleys were abandoned.

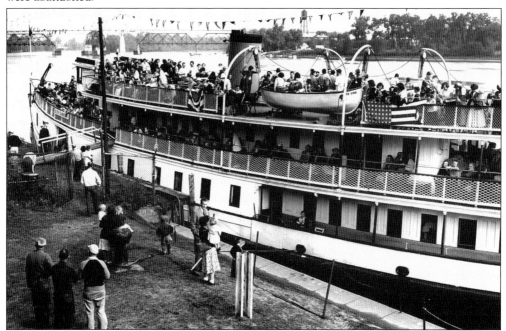

In this 1950s photograph, the ferryboat *Pemaquid* with its many passengers has arrived at Middletown's dock. The railroad and highway bridges can be seen upriver. Portland is at the upper right.

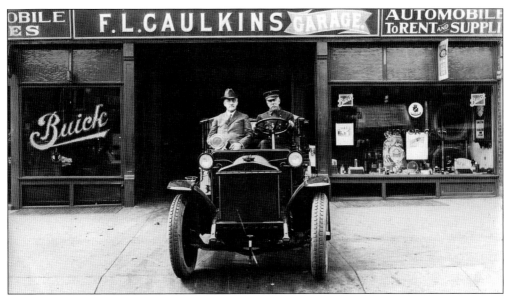

In 1903, furniture store owner Frederick L. Caulkins started selling automobiles. Two years later, he opened a showroom on Main Street. Of the early makes of cars sold by Caulkins, two are still produced today, the Buick and the Cadillac. In this c. 1915 photograph, Caulkins is joined by Middletown fire chief George Pitt (right) for a ride in a Federal Motor Company chemical engine.

The 1916 monthly statement of Durham buyer Mrs. Isbell reflects payments on her $1,026 bill. It is not recorded whether she purchased a Chalmers or a Buick. Several years earlier, Caulkins was selling Cadillacs for between $800 and $2,500.

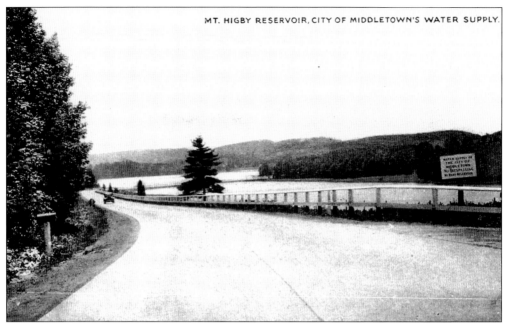

Built in 1897, the Mount Higby Reservoir provided much of Middletown's public water supply and still does so today. Located almost five miles west of downtown, it was built on 80 acres. Route 66, in this picture, cuts the reservoir in two and is still the main connector between Middletown and the city of Meriden to the west.

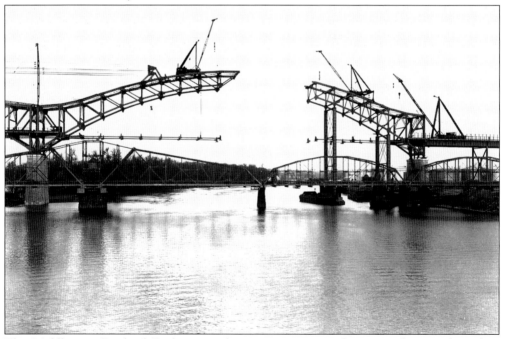

The Middletown–Portland Bridge is under construction in this 1937 photograph. When completed the following year, the bridge was the longest steel through arch bridge in the world. Years later it was renamed the Charles J. Arrigoni Bridge after the Durham state senator who was its main backer.

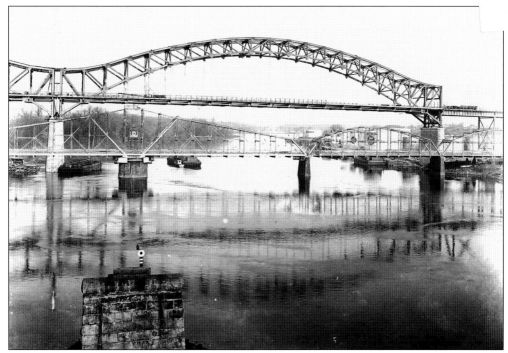

The short bridge pictured here was a draw bridge built in 1896. Towering over it in this 1938 shot is the bridge that would replace it in a few months, the Middletown–Portland Bridge. Today the 1938 bridge is still the means by which Middletown people cross the river by automobile and truck. Gov. Raymond Baldwin recalled years later that when the 1896 bridge was opened, it cost 2¢ to walk across to Portland and 7¢ to drive a horse and buggy over it with a passenger.

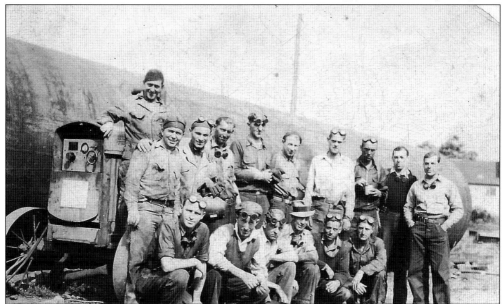

On October 8, 1936, construction workers take a break from the Middletown–Portland Bridge's construction to pose for this photograph. Made of steel and concrete, the new bridge would eventually cost $3.5 million to build.

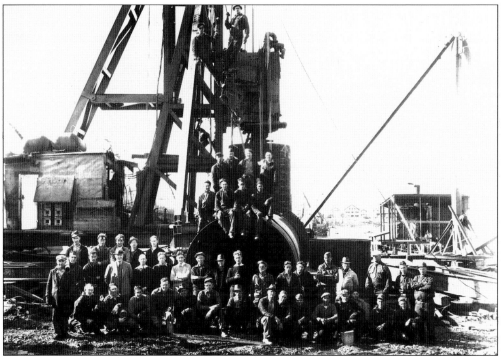

This photograph of the Middletown–Portland Bridge's construction crew was taken in 1937. The completed bridge would be 3,420 feet long and rest on three granite piers. The bridge deck would be 100 feet above the water, while the arches would be 100 feet above the deck. The construction of the bridge was completed without the loss of a single life.

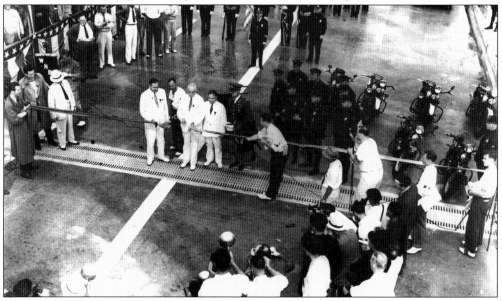

The much anticipated Middletown–Portland Bridge was dedicated on August 6, 1938. Approximately 50,000 people attended the ceremony. Gov. Wilbur L. Cross, seen in the white suit in the center, is cutting the ribbon. Samuel S. Mattes, the parade chairman, is at the right. State senator Charles J. Arrigoni from Durham, the bridge committee chairman, stands to the left.

Nine

DISASTERS

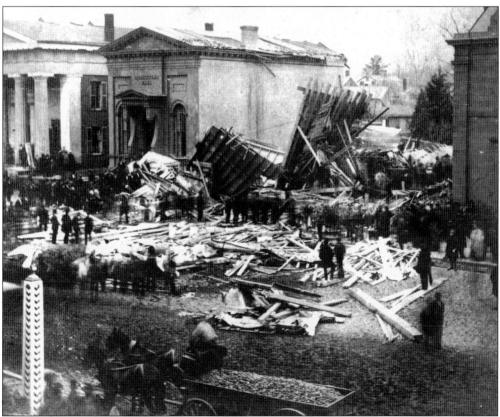

The Shepard Block, a three-story commercial brick building, was under construction on Main Street between the Middlwtown Custom House and the Middletown Bank. On April 10, 1873, at 4:00 p.m., it collapsed with 29 workers inside. Six men were killed in the one-minute-long collapse. Nine were injured. Hundreds of passersby helped to dig the trapped men out of the rubble. One man, C. W. Canfield, at work on the building's roof, fell with the collapsing bricks and wood but only suffered a small cut on his face.

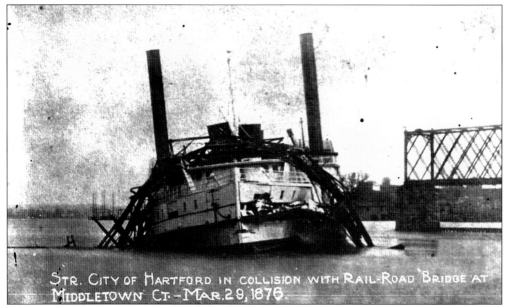

STR. CITY OF HARTFORD IN COLLISION WITH RAIL-ROAD BRIDGE AT MIDDLETOWN CT.—MAR. 29, 1876.

On March 29, 1876, the 24-year-old steamboat *City of Hartford* ran into the Middletown railroad bridge and broke off a 200-foot span from the west side of the bridge. Surviving this mishap, the boat was renamed *Capital City*, was placed back in service, and became irreparably damaged on rocks at Rye, New York, in 1886.

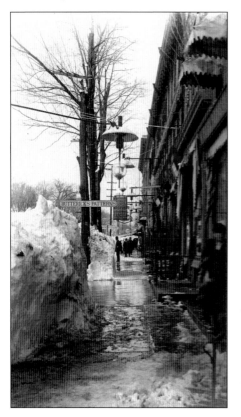

The great blizzard of 1888 hit in March with three days of heavy snow and biting winds from Washington, D.C., to Maine. The deepest snow accumulation in New England, 50 inches, was measured in Middletown. During the storm, business came to a halt, and people were prevented from leaving their homes.

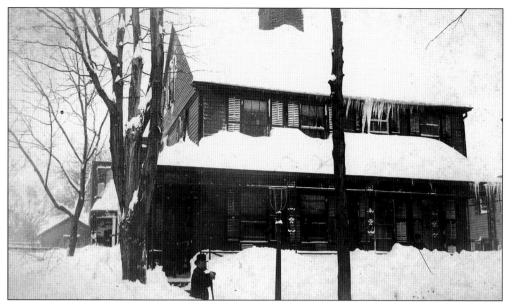

Stories of the blizzard of 1888 abounded, but the city did not fare as badly as the farms. After the storm had passed and shoveling was completed, folks got out their horses and sleighs and were amazed by the sights of the high drifts and white landscape.

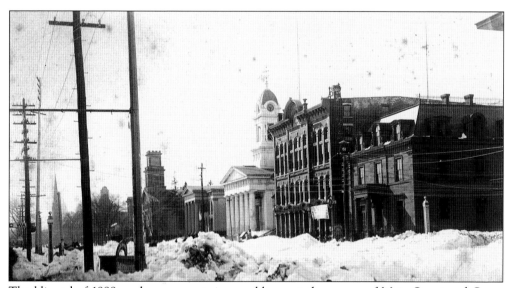

The blizzard of 1888 made some spots impassable, as at the corner of Main Street and Court Street. On the right side of this photograph, one can see, from right to left, the customhouse, the bank block, the courthouse, Nehemiah Hubbard's house, and the Universalist church with its square tower.

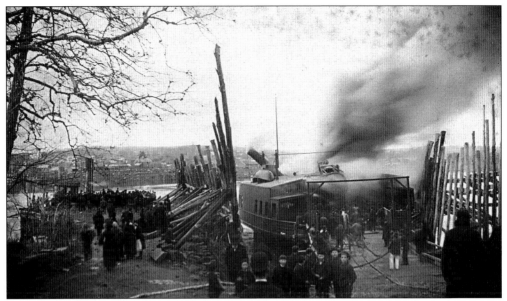

On April 2, 1889, the ferryboat *Portland*, built in 1870, caught fire and burned. Leaving Portand, the boat was about halfway across the river when flames shot out from around the smokestack. It made it to the slip on the Middletown side but, being beyond repair, was left to burn all afternoon.

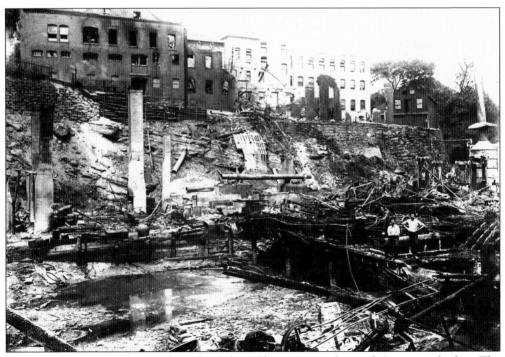

On July 31, 1907, fire destroyed much of the Wilcox, Crittenden and Company facility. The first company in the United States to manufacturer metal grommets, it was a mainstay of Middletown's manufacturing base. Company executives chose a new site two days later and were able to survive through the reconstruction without laying off any workers.

The most memorable hailstorm in Middletown history hit on September 11, 1912. This photograph was taken outside the offices of the *Penny Press*, the predecessor of the *Middletown Press* newspaper.

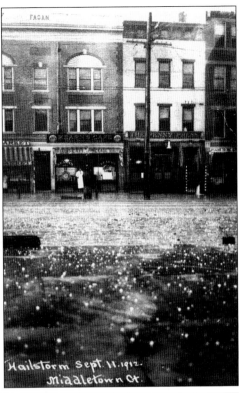

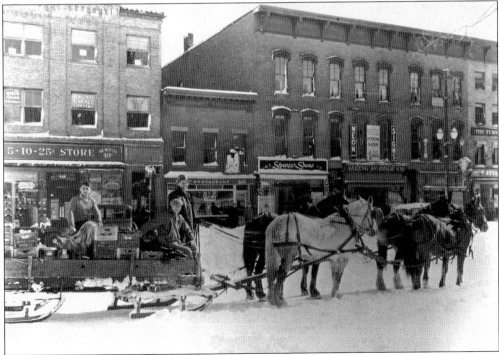

Taken in the aftermath of the blizzard of 1934, this picture shows, from left to right, Egidio Baraglia, Domenico Giuliano, and Lewis Daniels at the southeast corner of Main and Washington Streets.

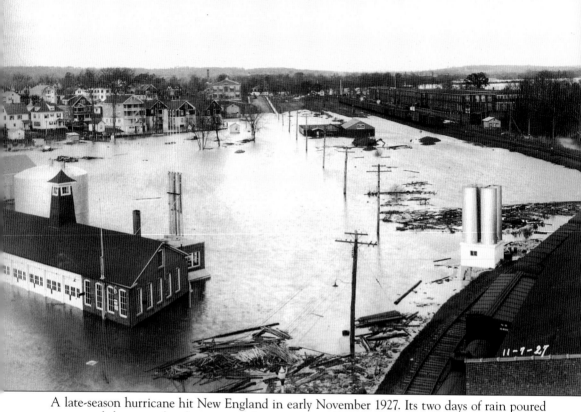

A late-season hurricane hit New England in early November 1927. Its two days of rain poured on ground that was already saturated from an unusually rainy October. The result was record flooding on much of the Connecticut River. Although Vermont and New Hampshire were the hardest hit, this November 7 photograph displays some of the flooding that hit Connecticut. Facing west from the site of the present Arrigoni Bridge, it shows much of the north end of Middletown under floodwaters. The location of North Main Street can only be determined by the tops of its telephone poles. To the right is the Noiseless Typewriter Company factory. Today the factory, the railroad tracks, and most of the homes in this photograph still exist, having escaped the revitalization activities that dramatically changed the south end of Middletown.

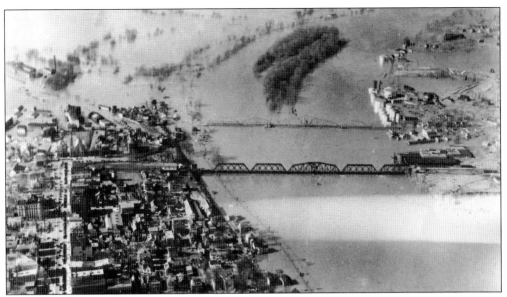

The 1936 flood brought ruin to many Connecticut businesses and people. For a half-century, the high-water mark was visible at the underpass to the highway by St. John's Catholic Church. St. John's can been seen near the top left in this photograph. Main Street is the wide street leading up the left side of this picture. It lies at a right angle to the railroad bridge. The thin strip between that bridge and Willow Island is the 1896 highway bridge. The flooded north meadows of Middletown are clearly shown in the upper left corner of this photograph. Portland's brownstone quarry, near the storage tanks at the top right in this photograph, ceased operation entirely after centuries of business, due to the 14 inches of rain and floodwater that flooded its basin.

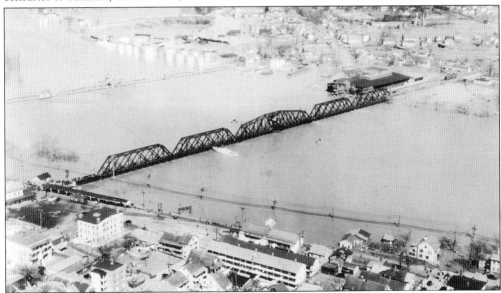

On March 12, 1936, the rain commenced and continued for nine days causing much hardship across New England. The river overflowed with rain, melted snow, and ice. It caused dams to burst, washing away homes, buildings, bridges, railways, and highways. There was some loss of life; thousands of Connecticut residents were left homeless. This photograph of the railroad bridge was taken by the U.S. Department of War.

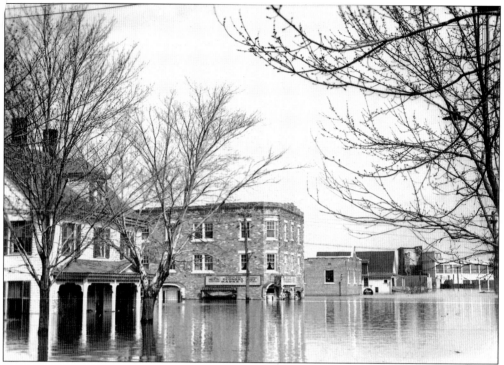

The 1936 flood caused damages of over $100 million, with the National Guard called in to assist during the paralyzing time. This photograph shows a flooded Stack Street and the North End Economy Market.

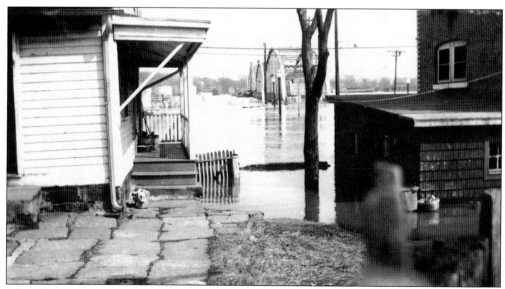

This photograph of the 1936 flood was taken from the River Road embankment at Miller Street. It looks at the 1896 highway bridge that would be replaced in two years by the new Middletown–Portland Bridge.

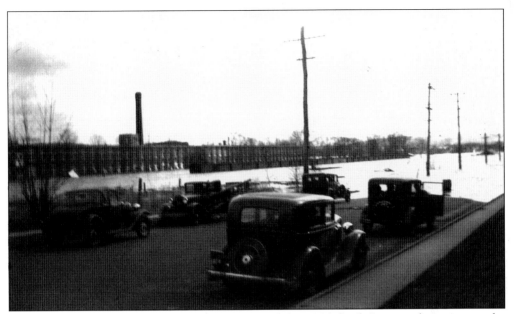

This picture shows cars stymied by the waters of the 1936 flood. It was taken next to the Remington Typewriter factory in Middletown's North End. This was the year that Remington closed Middletown's plant as the result of a contentious employee strike. It moved manufacturing operations to New York.

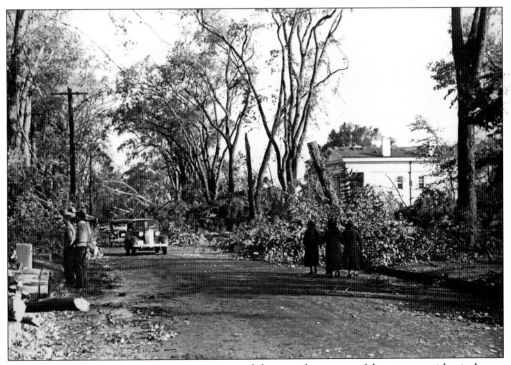

On September 21, 1938, Connecticut experienced the worst hurricane of the century with wind gusts of over 180 miles per hour. This photograph was taken on High Street just south of its intersection with Washington Street. The Samuel Wadsworth Russell House appears on the right.

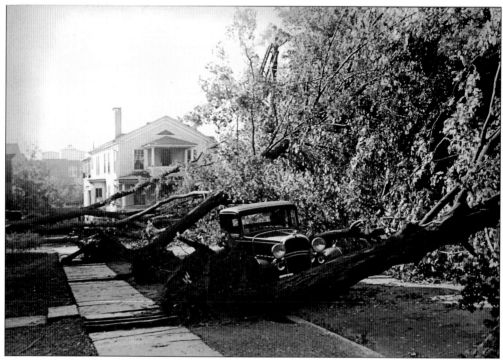

The winds, floods, tidal waves, and fires of the Hurricane of 1938 resulted in the deaths of 682 people. Connecticut experienced an unfortunate combination of nine inches of pre-storm rain, the autumnal equinox's high tides, and poor weather forecasting.

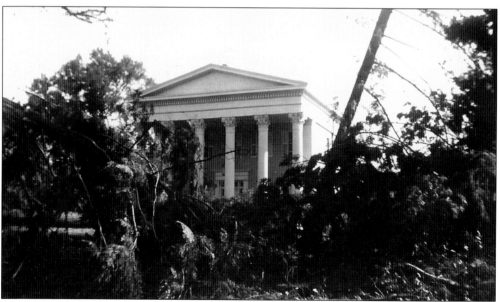

This photograph, taken in the aftermath of the Hurricane of 1938, shows huge piles of tree limbs in front of Wesleyan University's Russell House on High Street. The hurricane also pulled off the stone tower on Wesleyan University's chapel as well as the roofs of buildings housing 1,200 patients at the state mental hospital in Middletown's south end.

Ten

CELEBRATIONS AND SPEECHES

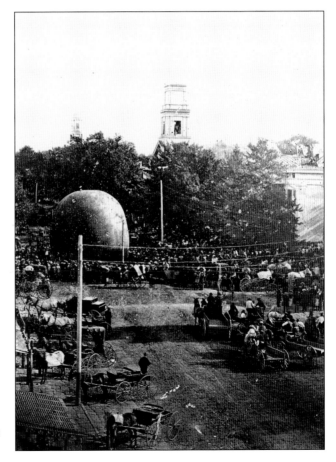

Many gathered to see this balloon ascension on the southern end of Main Street on September 2, 1863. Manned by celebrated balloonist Silas Brooks, the balloon took two hours to fill, finally rising at 4:00 p.m. This photograph captures the crowd, the tower of the Universalist church in the center, and the partially inflated balloon. As the balloon floated away, Brooks dropped handbills prepared by merchants S. Stearns and C. E. Putnam.

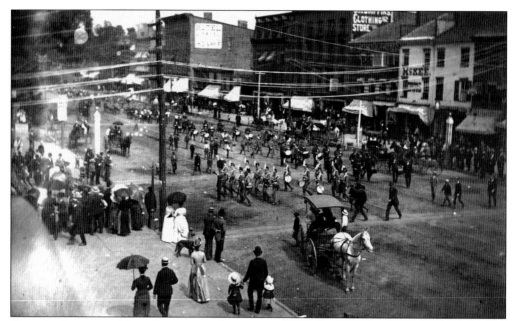

Since its inception, Main Street was where townsfolk gathered for parades. The town green at the south end of Main Street was an open area for rallies, meetings, music, and relaxation. Shown here is a parade on Main Street just north of Court Street about 1885. One can view the large electric light and the trolley tracks in the road along with the buildings across the street. These buildings are, from left to right, Hotel Chafee, J. H Griffins Clothing Store, a photograph shop, and McKee Drugs.

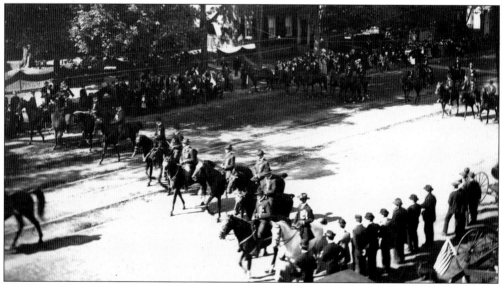

Middletown celebrated the 250th anniversary of its founding on October 11, 1900, with a three-mile-long parade of civic, military, and educational organizations. Extra trains from Hartford, New Haven, and Waterbury brought 25,000 visitors into town for the day. Parade participants included 56 Native Americans from Durham's Coginchaug tribe, the GAR Mansfield Post of Civil War veterans, fire companies, and company floats from Middletown and the surrounding communities.

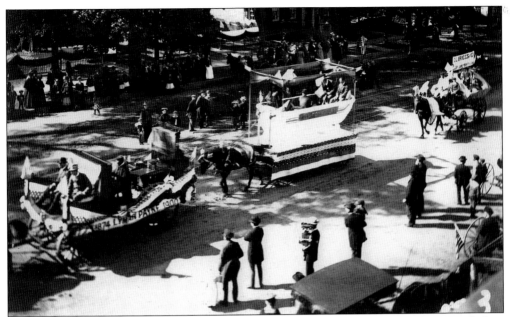

Many merchants participated in Middletown's 250th anniversary celebration of 1900 including (in the second wagon) Hale and Kelsey, a company that sold stoves, tinware, and plumbing on 314 Main Street. A patriotic banner of "1874 Lyman Payne 1900" adorns a wagon, as this dealer of pianos, organs, and other musical instruments captures viewers' attention by playing his piano while advertising his wares and reminding his customers that he is located at 279 Main Street.

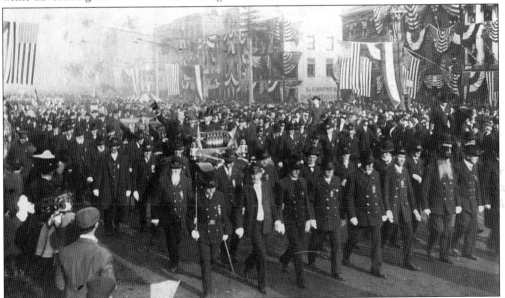

Middletown residents came out to join in a parade celebrating the visit of Pres. William Howard Taft and Vice Pres. James Sherman in 1909 on the occasion of the installation of a new Wesleyan University president. The parade, including 75 veterans of the Civil War, started on Bridge Street, passed 400 singing schoolchildren near St. John's Parochial School, proceeded down Main Street, circled Union Park, and stopped at Middlesex Theater where the president's party disembarked for the installation exercises.

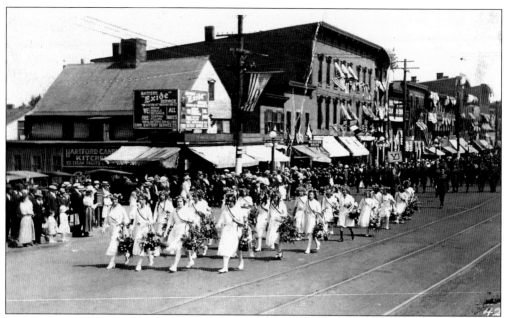

Middletown's Welcome Home Day Parade on May 30, 1919, celebrated the sacrifices of the soldiers of World War I. Schoolgirls march in front as the servicemen are seen to the right. The World War I monument on Washington Green lists 37 Middletown men who died in the service of their country during 1917–1918.

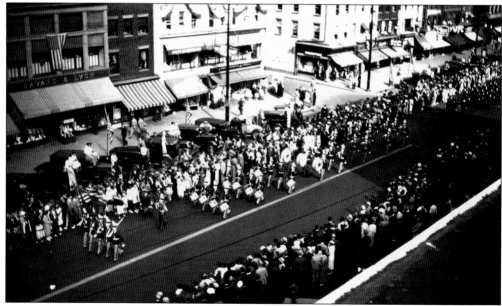

This photograph shows Connecticut's 300th anniversary in 1935. On May 25, 1935, the past came alive as historical floats, costumed figures, animals, cars, veterans, and marching bands participated in Connecticut's tercentenary parade. Sears Roebuck is seen here at its original site near the corner of Main Street and Court Street. Later it moved to a larger, newly constructed building just down the street closer to the river, which provided its customers much-needed additional parking.

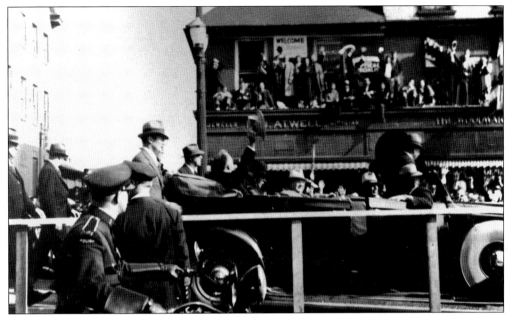

On October 22, 1936, Pres. Franklin D. Roosevelt and an entourage of 60 motor vehicles made a one-day marathon campaign trip through Connecticut. He visited Hartford, Middletown, Meriden, Waterbury, Naugatuck, Seymour, Ansonia, New Haven, Bridgeport, Westport, Norwalk, and Stamford, speaking at each location except Seymour. Here he is seen waving to the rooftop crowds on Main Street in Middletown. Two weeks later, Roosevelt was reelected to his second term as president of the United States.

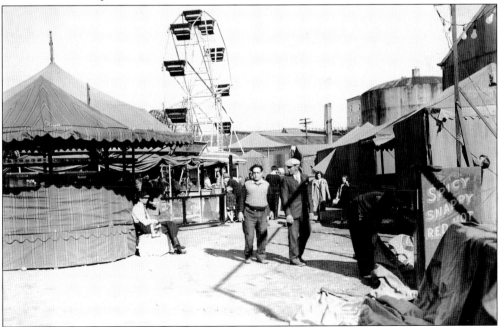

This 1938 carnival was at the north end of Middletown. The city is no stranger to carnivals, having been the home of Coleman Brothers Carnival's winter headquarters for many years. Each season, Palmer Field is the first stop for the Coleman tour of northeastern fairgrounds.

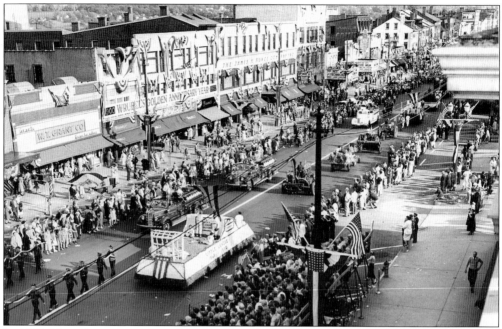

In 1950, Main Street was festooned with patriotic flags and banners as Middletown celebrated its 300th anniversary. Its citizens proudly viewed floats, marching bands, and dignitaries. This bustling street had many shops including Wrubel's Department Store, which was celebrating its 50th anniversary. The American flag flying in the foreground has 48 stars, and it would be almost another decade before statehood for Alaska and Hawaii would add more stars.

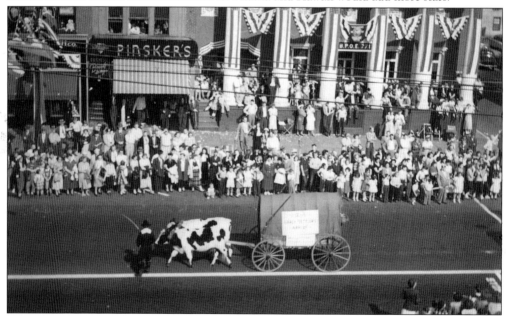

The Middlesex County Historical Society float passes the Elks lodge and Pinsker's jewelry store in the Middletown Tercentenary Parade on September 16, 1950. Leroy Post of Portland was the driver in costume. L. B. Markham was chairman of the float committee, and Joseph Repozo of Portland provided the steers and wagon.

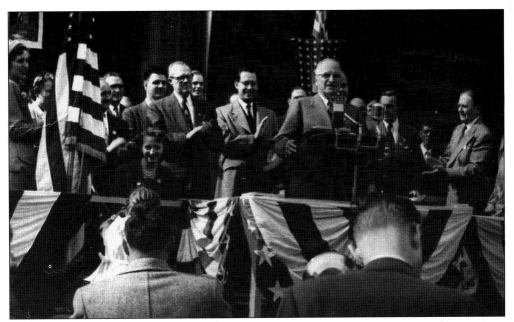

On October 16, 1952, outgoing president Harry Truman made a campaign visit to Connecticut. Accompanied by his daughter, Margaret, on the left and Congressman Abraham Ribicoff on the right, Truman voiced support for Democratic presidential candidate Adlai Stevenson. Truman also praised his own secretary of state, Middletown native Dean Acheson, stating that he had developed a program that had "stopped Communism in its tracks." Although crowd reaction was mixed, a majority of the 10,000 people present were Truman supporters.

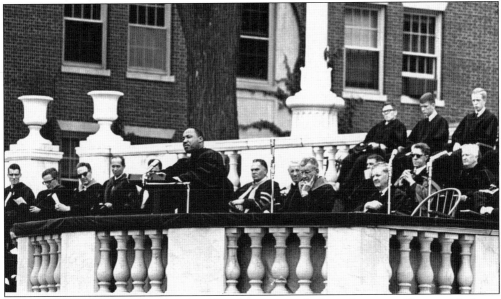

In this photograph, Dr. Martin Luther King Jr. is giving the baccalaureate address at Wesleyan University on June 7, 1964. He is standing at Denison Terrace, which lies between the Olin Memorial Library and Andrus Field. Less than a month later, he would attend the signing of the Civil Rights Act of 1964, and six months later he would receive the Nobel Peace Prize. (Courtesy Wesleyan University.)

BIBLIOGRAPHY

Baldwin, Raymond L. *Reminiscences of Middletown*. Middletown, CT: Middlesex County Historical Society, 1969.

Cunningham, Janice P., and Elizabeth A. Warner. *Experiment in Community: An African American Neighborhood, Middletown, Connecticut, 1847–1930*. Middletown, CT: Connecticut Historical Commission, 2002.

Delaney, Edmund. *The Connecticut River, New England's Historic Waterway*. Chester, CT: Globe Pequot Press, 1983.

———. *Life in the Connecticut River Valley, 1800–1840: From the Recollections of John Howard Redfield*. Essex, CT: Connecticut River Museum, 1988.

Hallock, Frank K., and James L. McConaughy. *A Pamphlet Containing Two Articles on Middletown and the Connecticut River*. Middletown, CT: Middlesex County Historical Society, 1950.

Halloran, Frances W., and Betty Turco. *Middletown, Connecticut Vignettes: In Celebration of the Nation's Bicentennial*. Middletown, CT: Middletown Commission on the Arts and Cultural Activities, 1976.

Hubbard, Josiah Meigs. *Two and a Half Centuries of Farm Life in Middletown, Connecticut*. Middletown, CT: Middlesex County Historical Society, 1907.

The Leading Business Men of Middletown, Portland, Durham and Middlefield. Boston: Mercantile Publishing Company, 1890.

Ossad, Steven L., and Don R. Marsh. *Major General Maurice Rose, World War II's Greatest Forgotten Commander*. New York: Taylor Trade Publishing, 2003.

Snow, Wilbert. *Codline's Child: The Autobiography of Wilbert Snow*. Middletown, CT: Wesleyan University Press, 1974.

Tuttle, Sam. *Picture Book of Old Connecticut*. Scotia, NY: Americana Review, 1979.

Van Dusen, Albert E. *Middletown and the American Revolution*. Middletown, CT: Middlesex County Historical Society, 1976.

Wallace, Willard M. *Middletown: 1650–1950*. Middletown, CT: City of Middletown, 1950.

Warner, Elizabeth A. *A Pictorial History of Middletown*. Middletown, CT: Great Middletown Preservation, 1990.

INDEX

ACROSS AMERICA, PEOPLE ARE DISCOVERING SOMETHING WONDERFUL. *THEIR HERITAGE.*

Arcadia Publishing is the leading local history publisher in the United States. With more than 3,000 titles in print and hundreds of new titles released every year, Arcadia has extensive specialized experience chronicling the history of communities and celebrating America's hidden stories, bringing to life the people, places, and events from the past. To discover the history of other communities across the nation, please visit:

www.arcadiapublishing.com

Customized search tools allow you to find regional history books about the town where you grew up, the cities where your friends and family live, the town where your parents met, or even that retirement spot you've been dreaming about.

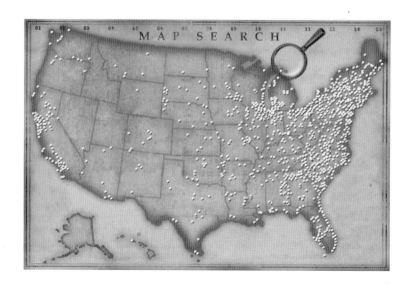